A Pyramid Cooking Paperback

Gluten-free
cooking

Lyndel Costain
& Joanna Farrow

hamlyn

Lyndel Costain B.Sc.SRD is an award-winning state registered dietitian, health writer, and broadcaster on television and radio. She is passionate about the importance of correctly diagnosing and treating the often overlooked condition of gluten intolerance (or celiac disease). Lyndel has 20 years experience, is a past spokesperson for the British Dietetic Association, and regularly writes for professional and popular books and magazines.

Joanna Farrow trained as a home economist and worked for several years on women's magazines. She is now a freelance writer and works for a range of food magazines including *BBC Good Food*. Joanna has written a diverse range of cookery books and also styles food for photography.

An Hachette UK Company
www.hachette.co.uk

A Pyramid Paperback

First published in Great Britain in 2005 by Hamlyn,
a division of Octopus Publishing Group Ltd
Endeavour House
189 Shaftesbury Avenue
London
WC2H 8JY
www.octopusbooksusa.com

This revised edition published 2010

Distributed in the U.S. and Canada by Octopus Books USA:
c/o Hachette Book Group
237 Park Avenue
New York, NY 10017

This material was first published as *Gluten-free Food*

ISBN 978-0-600-62086-0

Printed and bound in China

10 9 8 7 6 5 4 3 2 1

NOTES
All the recipes in this book have been analyzed by a professional nutritionist. Nutritional analysis provided is per serving. The calcium and iron content may vary if non-dairy alternatives are used in place of dairy milk, butter, and cream.

This books includes dishes made with nuts and nut derivatives. It is advisable for those with known allergic reactions to nuts and nut derivatives and those who may be potentially vulnerable to these allergies, such as pregnant and nursing mothers, invalids, the elderly, babies, and children, to avoid dishes made with nuts and nut oils. It is also prudent to check the labels of prepared ingredients for the possible inclusion of nut derivatives.

CONTENTS

Introduction

Following a gluten-free diet means you will always have to choose and cook gluten-free food.

This book offers practical help for anyone who suffers from gluten intolerance. It gives clear advice on how to ensure accurate diagnosis of symptoms, and explains how you can continue to enjoy a healthy and varied diet. Most importantly, it provides a comprehensive guide for people with celiac disease, which is a lifelong, genetically linked condition that can affect people of any age, sex, or ethnicity. If the problem is not treated with a strict gluten-free diet, it can have serious and wide-ranging health implications. It is also much more common than was once thought and is greatly under-diagnosed.

Anyone who has had to change their diet for health reasons will know what an impact this has on day-to-day life. You will need to check and be sure of everything you eat and friends and family will also need to understand the importance and practicalities of the changes involved. It is important to check that ready-made ingredients such as mustard, ketchup, soy sauce, chocolate, and stock are gluten-free (and gluten-free foods are also wheat-free if following a wheat-free diet).

Before you even reach this stage, actually identifying gluten intolerance can be hard work. Food intolerance is a difficult area, partly because of a limited understanding of the subject and partly because of the lack of reliable food intolerance tests. People may spend a lot of time and money looking for an answer to their health problems, without finding effective help and possibly compromising their nutritional intake in the process.

However, the good news is that there are clear diagnostic tests for celiac disease. There are also sensible, safe ways to investigate wheat allergy and intolerance. This book will give you the confidence to assess and deal with your symptoms. It also provides an extensive range of mouthwatering recipes to ensure that your tastebuds never have to suffer. This means you will be in a position to take charge of your own health and well-being—for life.

The five main food groups required for a balanced diet

Fruit and
vegetables

Bread, cereals,
and potatoes

Meat, fish,
and other
protein foods

Milk and
dairy foods

Fats, oils, and
sugary foods

This chart shows the five food groups that contribute to a balanced
and varied diet in the healthiest proportions. By choosing suitable
foods from each group every day, you will get the nutrients you need.

SYMBOLS USED IN THIS BOOK

gluten-free

wheat-free

cows'
milk-free

egg-free

nut-free

suitable for
vegetarians

Adverse reactions to food

FOOD ALLERGY

Some people, described as being "atopic," produce excessive amounts of an antibody called immunoglobulin E (IgE) when they eat or inhale allergens, which could be certain foods (such as milk, nuts, fish, and eggs), pollens, dust, or animal fur. This rapidly causes allergic reactions such as a runny nose, wheezing, urticaria (hives or nettle rash), flushing, swelling of the face, or, in extreme cases, life-threatening anaphylaxis. Atopic people can have delayed reactions to foods, when symptoms such as eczema, asthma, diarrhea, or migraine do not appear for several hours or days.

It is also possible to have food allergies that are not triggered by IgE antibodies but by other parts of the immune system. The best-known example of this type of food allergy is celiac disease, a condition in which the bowel reacts adversely to gluten.

FOOD INTOLERANCE

Food intolerance causes allergic reactions that do not involve the immune system. There are a number of different types:

- **Enzyme problems** For example when people lack lactase, the enzyme that digests lactose, the sugar found in milk. People with celiac disease may have lactose intolerance (see page 36).
- **Food aversion** This is where people avoid a food either for psychological reasons or because they link it to feeling ill. For example, if someone was coincidentally very sick after eating a certain food, they may be put off eating that food again.
- **Ingredient or chemical sensitivity** Certain substances in food can provoke symptoms in susceptible people. For example, tyramine in matured cheese and red wine may cause migraine or flushing, and the preservative sulfur dioxide may aggravate asthma.
- **Other causes** For example, wheat intolerance. There is much debate about whether proteins in some foods make the bowel lining "leaky," allowing them to enter the bloodstream and cause symptoms. Upsetting the natural balance of bacteria in the bowel may also have a role to play in understanding food intolerance.

Some people have unpleasant allergic reactions when they eat certain foods.

Gluten and celiac disease

WHAT IS GLUTEN?

Celiac disease is caused by the body reacting badly to gluten, a type of protein found predominantly in wheat. Gluten becomes sticky and malleable when combined with water, meaning that it is ideal for bread-making. Gluten itself comprises many different proteins, the best-known of which is gliadin. This is the part of gluten that triggers the immune reaction. Proteins in rye, barley, and possibly oats (see page 18) are very similar to gliadin and they too damage the bowel of people with celiac disease.

In the case of wheat allergy, the body also reacts badly to the different proteins found in wheat. However, these proteins have not been as well researched and identified as the proteins that trigger celiac disease and the related skin condition dermatitis herpetiformis (see page 8).

Gluten is a type of protein found predominantly in wheat and barley.

WHEN DID GLUTEN INTOLERANCE START?

Human beings have been on earth for many thousands of years, but for most of this time they were hunters and gatherers, trapping animals, catching fish, and collecting wild vegetables, fruit, seeds, and herbs. Only quite recently in evolutionary terms—about 10,000 years ago—did groups of our ancestors learn how to domesticate plants and animals, and as a result form stable, permanent settlements.

This was the beginning of agriculture, and would have seen the first appearance of crops of gluten-containing wheat and barley. It would also have seen the first appearance of what we know today as celiac disease. For some reason, certain people were not able to tolerate this new protein in their diet.

As agriculture became established around the world, only populations that grew wheat and barley were affected in this way. Large areas of the world where rice, corn, millet, and sorghum were the main grains would have been, and still are, essentially, unaffected. But as our populations move and intermingle, so the genetic potential for celiac disease increases.

Celiac disease explained

Sufferers must avoid (clockwise from top left) barley, wheat, rye, and possibly oats in their diet.

Celiac disease is a genetically linked condition caused by a lifelong intolerance to gluten in wheat and similar proteins in rye, barley, and possibly oats. When people with celiac disease eat gluten-containing foods, their immune system fights the gluten, causing inflammation of the delicate cells lining the small intestine. In the process, the small intestine's villi—finger-like projections that absorb nutrients and fluid from food and drink—become flattened and cannot do their job, causing digestive and nutritional upsets.

WHO GETS CELIAC DISEASE?

Celiac disease is most common in areas where a lot of wheat is eaten. In America and some European countries, for example, it affects 1 percent of the population. Celiac disease runs in families and can begin at any age, even if the person has previously eaten gluten without problem. In addition, some sort of trigger, such as a bad accident, a viral infection, or even pregnancy, may set it off.

DERMATITIS HERPETIFORMIS

Dermatitis herpetiformis (DH) results in itchy blisters mainly on the back of the elbows and forearms, the buttocks, and the front of the knees. In the 1960s it was shown that people with DH also have a very mild form of celiac disease and a gluten-free diet is prescribed as treatment. This may take up to 6 months to have an effect, however, so medication may also be used for a few months.

Celiac disease is most common in countries where wheat-based foods are eaten.

DH is investigated by examining the skin for immunoglobulin A (IgA). Diagnosis is confirmed using the tests for celiac disease (see page 11). It is a lifelong condition with a genetic basis, but is much rarer than celiac disease, affecting about one in 15,000 people. It is possible for celiac disease sufferers to develop DH, but the risk is greatly decreased if they follow a gluten-free diet.

Symptoms

The symptoms of celiac disease can vary greatly or may be missed, which is why so many people remain undiagnosed. The most common are diarrhea, tiredness, anemia, bloating, wind, low mood, and weight loss, all of which may come and go.

Some babies who have been healthy from birth may become irritable, anemic, and fail to grow properly once gluten-containing cereals are introduced. Others may have problems when they are toddlers. Diarrhea, a potbelly, and passing smelly, pale stools that are difficult to flush away are other common signs.

In the past, the condition was recognized only when people were ill. These days, "silent" cases (with no obvious symptoms) are sometimes picked up during blood tests for, say, anemia or irritable bowel syndrome. Once people with "silent" celiac disease start a gluten-free diet, they usually feel more energetic.

Celiac disease is also linked to other health problems. The list on the right shows the conditions that could develop if celiac disease remains untreated (note, though, that there are also other reasons why these conditions might develop).

CAN CELIAC DISEASE BE PREVENTED?

When celiac disease was first recognized, it was seen largely as a problem for young children, but since the mid-1970s fewer children and more adults have been diagnosed. This is thought to be because more women are breast-feeding their babies (helping to strengthen the bowel and immune system), and also because more babies are being weaned onto gluten-free foods. Babies' immune systems are quite fragile in the first few months and gluten could trigger celiac disease if they are genetically predisposed.

Recent research found that the risk of celiac disease was reduced by 40 percent in children under two if they were still breast-fed when first given gluten-containing foods. The reduction increased to 65 percent if they continued to be breast-fed while having gluten-containing foods. However, these studies do not tell us if celiac disease was eliminated or simply postponed.

Related conditions
The following are conditions that may develop if celiac disease is left untreated:
- Mouth ulcers
- Sore tongue
- Nausea, poor appetite
- Stomach pain
- Vitamin and mineral deficiencies
- Depression and anxiety
- Weak bones (osteoporosis)
- Cramps
- Rheumatoid arthritis
- Hair loss
- Weakened tooth enamel
- Susceptibility to infections
- Easy bruising
- Difficulty getting pregnant
- Repeated miscarriage
- Not reaching full height potential
- Skin problems such as psoriasis and eczema
- Liver disease
- Tingling in the hands and feet
- Epilepsy
- Ataxia (a disorder of the nervous system)
- Psychiatric disturbances

Investigation and treatment

We have already seen that celiac disease is under-diagnosed, but it is still the case that much more is known about it than about wheat intolerance. In fact, some nutritionists are not sure if wheat intolerance, as distinct from gluten intolerance, exists. Since the two share some common symptoms—tiredness, low mood, and bowel upsets, for example—it is quite possible that what people think of as wheat intolerance is actually celiac disease. This makes it absolutely vital to ensure that celiac disease is properly diagnosed and then treated with a gluten-free, not just a wheat-free, diet to protect future health.

If you suspect that you or a member of your family reacts badly to wheat, then your first step should be to see your doctor. It really helps to take along a food and symptom diary (see below). Based on your general health, medical history, and food diary, your doctor will be able to make decisions about whether wheat allergy or intolerance or celiac disease is your problem. If wheat allergy—where the immune system is involved—is suspected, you can be referred for medical food allergy tests. If positive, the results will need confirming with a medically supervised wheat challenge. You will then need to follow a wheat-free diet (see page 15).

When it comes to wheat intolerance, there are at present no medical tests that give a reliable diagnosis. You will have to try removing wheat from your diet and noting how your symptoms change. Unorthodox approaches such as hair analysis, pulse tests, sweat tests, and kinesiology have no proven scientific basis and are not recommended by health professionals.

Bread is the most common source of wheat in the diet.

FOOD AND SYMPTOM DIARY

If you suspect that food containing wheat upsets you in some way, keep a food and symptom diary for a few weeks to get a clearer picture. Fill the diary in throughout the day, as it is very hard to remember what you have eaten after the event. Record absolutely everything you eat and drink, including any medicines and supplements.

INVESTIGATING CELIAC DISEASE

You should talk to your doctor about being tested for celiac disease if:

- You seem to react badly to wheat.
- You have been suffering from any or a number of the symptoms described on page 9 and there is no other medically confirmed reason for them, or you are not feeling better after being treated for a medical reason.
- Someone in your family has celiac disease, even if you do not have any symptoms.
- You have Type 1 diabetes (see page 35).

Seek advice from your doctor if you think you may be suffering from celiac disease.

There are two types of test used to investigate and diagnose celiac disease. First, there are blood tests that look for specific antibodies. You must ensure that you have eaten a normal gluten-containing diet for a couple of weeks leading up to the test. If the tests are positive, it is very likely, though not definite, that you have celiac disease. Occasionally, antibody tests on people who have celiac disease appear normal (a false negative test) while those on people who do not have it show raised antibody levels (a false positive test). To help make sense of the tests, your doctor will also look for other common problems, such as anemia. If all of the above tests are negative but your symptoms persist, it is wise to be retested in the future. This is especially important for children.

A second test is required for a final and definite diagnosis. A gastroenterologist will carry out a quick and painless biopsy of the small intestine. If damage is found, celiac disease is confirmed.

INVESTIGATING WHEAT INTOLERANCE

Celiac disease should always be ruled out before commencing a wheat-free diet. However, if you have reactions that take hours or days to develop, or are always present, and you feel that wheat may be responsible, you can investigate using this approach:

- Follow a wheat-free diet for three weeks. If you have any other medical problems, check with your doctor first. You may also benefit from the help of a qualified dietitian.

- Plan ahead to ensure that you have the right foods in the house and choose a time when it is easiest from a social point of view to follow the diet. Keep up your food and symptom diary.
- If there is no improvement in your symptoms, then wheat intolerance is unlikely to be the problem. However, celiac disease (or another food allergy/intolerance) is still a possibility, so discuss this with your doctor.
- If your symptoms improve or disappear, then reintroduce wheat* to see if they come back—this is known as a wheat challenge (see below). If they do return, then wheat intolerance is possible. However, so is celiac disease.
- Make an appointment to see your doctor to discuss whether or not you have celiac disease. Take along your food and symptom diary. If wheat intolerance is diagnosed, then you will need to follow a wheat-free diet (see page 15). If celiac disease is your problem, you will need a gluten-free diet.

WHEAT CHALLENGE

- Retry wheat for at least three days—or for a week if eczema and migraine are your symptoms.
- Any foods that are 100 percent wheat are suitable: for example, 100 percent wheat pasta, cereal, or crackers.
- Eat a little more of the food every day.
- If you have no reaction, then keep eating the food. If you have a reaction, stop eating it and arrange to see your doctor.

*Food challenges should never be attempted with children, or if there is any risk or history of anaphylaxis, without medical supervision.

TREATMENT

This book should always be used in addition to the advice you get from your dietitian and doctor rather than being seen as an alternative. Lifestyles differ and people have different dietary and medical requirements. Your dietitian will be able to provide advice that is tailored to your situation and will know how to answer your specific questions. They will also have information about support groups.

100 percent wheat foods, such as pasta, are the most suitable for a "wheat challenge."

Once the diagnosis of celiac disease or dermatitis herpetiformis (see page 8) is confirmed, your gastroenterologist will refer you to a dietitian who will explain the principles and importance of a gluten-free diet and give practical guidance on following it on a day-to-day basis. If you have celiac disease you will need to follow your diet for life, even when you feel well. A lack of obvious symptoms does not mean that gluten is not affecting the bowel and so increasing the risk of health problems.

Most people with obvious symptoms find that they start to feel better within days of beginning their gluten-free diet. Lost weight is gradually regained—sometimes very quickly, as improved well-being means a bigger appetite—and energy levels increase, regardless of how healthy they felt beforehand.

If you continue to feel unwell after a few weeks, it is likely that you are still getting some gluten in your diet. This could be by accident or simply because you are finding it hard to go without some favorite foods. However, if you feel sure that you are following your diet carefully, do speak to your doctor.

Your dietitian will be able to advise you about the need for any vitamin and mineral supplements, together with any other necessary dietary changes: for example, if you also have lactose intolerance (see page 36). Remember, once you start the gluten-free diet, the bowel heals and starts to absorb food and nutrients properly, and problems like lactose intolerance typically resolve.

Most people with celiac disease soon regain any lost weight once they start a gluten-free diet.

HAVE REGULAR CHECKUPS

In the first year of diagnosis, it is sensible to have three or four checkups with your doctor and, if possible, your dietitian. It helps if close family members visit at some point too, so that they also understand the importance and practicalities of the gluten-free diet. Thereafter, aim to have checkups once or twice a year, to make sure you are staying well and are following your diet carefully.

Symptoms may flare up in times of stress or change—pregnancy is a common time for women (see page 26)—so seek regular advice from your doctor and dietitian at these times.

Ensure your diet is gluten-free

When you have celiac disease, enjoying a varied gluten-free diet is vital for good health, but it does take practice, vigilance, and creativity. You must be extremely careful about what you buy for lunch at school or work, what you eat at dinner parties or in restaurants, and what you do when you feel hungry.

As you will see from the table on page 16, most of our basic foods, such as meat, fish, eggs, vegetables, fruit, and dairy products, are naturally gluten-free. Gluten is found only in wheat, barley, rye, and possibly oats. So following a gluten-free diet means knowing how to avoid everything that contains these grains and their products, notably flour. Wheat flour is the richest and most common source of gluten and as well as occurring in obvious sources such as bread, pasta, and cookies, it is used in many processed foods, often in different guises. For example, some gluten-containing ingredients do not contain the word "wheat" (see left), labeling laws can mean that not all ingredients actually appear on the food label. From January 2006, however, manufacturers have had to state whether food contains wheat.

Even if you feel quite well after eating gluten, it could still affect the bowel, so try to resist temptation for your health's sake. Be sure to take official gluten-free food directories when shopping, look for "gluten-free" symbols, and read labels carefully. The good news is that special pens that test for the presence of gluten are currently being developed and should help to increase food choices and prevent mistakes.

BEWARE CONTAMINATION

As well as avoiding all the obvious sources, it is important to ensure that your gluten-free foods are not "contaminated" by others that contain gluten. For example, store-bought meringues are likely to have come into contact with gluten-containing cakes, while takeout French fries may have met with batter in the deep-fat fryer. Also, never share breadboards, toasters, or butter dishes with users of standard bread.

Hidden ingredients
On food labels, the following ingredients may contain gluten:
- Barley, pot or Scotch barley
- Bran
- Bread crumbs
- Bulgar or cracked wheat
- Cereal extract
- Couscous
- Cracker meal
- Farina
- Flour, whole-wheat flour, wheat flour
- Gluten
- Modified starch
- Rolled oats, oatmeal, porridge oats
- Rusk
- Rye flour
- Semolina
- Spelt, kamut
- Vegetable protein, vegetable gum, vegetable starch
- Wheat bran, wheat germ, wheat starch
- Whole-wheat, wheat

Following a wheat-free diet

Celiac disease should always be ruled out before following a wheat-free diet. Those with a medically diagnosed wheat allergy or intolerance will need to follow a diet that excludes wheat and all foods containing wheat flour and wheat-derived ingredients. However, unlike celiac disease, which is a lifelong condition, wheat intolerance may be transient. Young children may "grow out" of wheat allergy by school-age. If you or your child suffers from wheat intolerance, retry wheat every six months or so (see page 12).

DIAGNOSING WHEAT INTOLERANCE

The symptoms of wheat intolerance and celiac disease are often similar, such as bowel upsets, tiredness, and bloating, so it can be difficult to tell them apart. Also, if people with either condition cut wheat from their diet, they are likely to feel better (see page 10).

A WHEAT-FREE DIET

A wheat-free diet can include rye, barley, and oats, meaning that you can eat rye bread and crackers, barley in soups and casseroles, oat cakes and oatmeal. Specially manufactured gluten-free foods such as flour mixes and pasta, may be made from deglutenized wheat, which is unsuitable for wheat-free diets.

Wheat is also "hidden" in many foods, so you need to look for hidden ingredients when shopping or eating away from home:

- Always read ingredients lists on food labels.
- Check processed foods in wheat-free food guides supplied by supermarkets.
- Avoid contamination from breadboards, toasters, and bakeries.
- When eating away from home, check that ingredients are wheat-free (in advance if possible); if in doubt, avoid them.
- Take wheat-free meals with you if you are unsure about availability.
- Use this book, collect other recipes, and make use of information from wheat-free food manufacturers.
- Seek your dietitian's advice to ensure nutritional adequacy and to help you recheck whether your wheat intolerance still exists.

Ingredients to avoid
- Bran, wheat bran, wheat germ
- Cereal filler, cereal binder, cereal protein
- Farina
- Flour, whole-wheat flour, wheat flour, wheat starch
- Rusk
- Starch, modified starch, edible starch
- Vegetable protein, vegetable gum, vegetable starch
- Wheat, durum wheat, semolina, couscous, spelt, bulgar/cracked wheat

Pure rye breads and crackers are suitable for a wheat-free diet.

Choosing gluten-free foods

Food type	Foods allowed	Foods to avoid/check
Cereals/grains	Corn, all types of rice, sorghum, sago, millet, tapioca, buckwheat, teff, quinoa, rice bran	Wheat, barley, rye, spelt, triticale, kamut, bulgar wheat, couscous, durum wheat, semolina, wheat bran, oats,* oat bran*
Flours	Rice, corn, soy, potato, chestnut, maize, gram, chick pea/channa, sorghum, tapioca	All types of wheat, rye, and oat* flour
Breakfast cereals	Any made from permitted cereals	Any made using wheat, rye, barley, oats*
Baked foods, pasta	Gluten-free breads, cookies, crispbreads, cakes, pastries, flour mix, pasta	Conventional breads, cakes, cookies, rusks, pastries, crispbreads, pasta, ice-cream cones
Meat, poultry, fish, and eggs	All plain-cooked varieties and when used in dishes/products with gluten-free ingredients	Savory pies, pasties, sausages, crumbed, battered, stuffed, and processed products
Milk and milk products; soy	Milk, most yogurts, cream, most cheeses; soy milks, yogurts, and cheeses; tofu	Yogurt with crunchy ingredients; some artificial creams and processed cheeses
Fats	Butter, margarine, oils, lard, dripping	Suet, some brands of low-fat spread

* Research now suggests that some people with celiac disease can safely eat moderate amounts of uncontaminated oats (see page 18), but check with your doctor or dietitian before including them in your diet.

Food type	Foods allowed	Foods to avoid/check
Vegetables	All types: fresh, frozen, dried, juiced (check ingredients if canned or in ready-made salads or bean and vegetable dishes)	Vegetables in sauce or dressing made using wheat flour; crumbed or battered vegetables; potato waffles and croquettes
Fruit	All types: fresh, frozen, dried, juiced, canned	Some fruit-pie fillings
Soups, sauces	All types thickened/made with gluten-free ingredients; some canned and dried soups	Gravy mixes, soups, and sauces made with non-permitted flour or pasta
Desserts	Gelatin, milk, or soy desserts made from gluten-free cereals; some ice creams, sorbets, and mousses	Desserts made using wheat flour, semolina, bread crumbs, oats*, or suet
Snack foods	Plain nuts and seeds, some brands of chips, savory snacks, dips, candies and chocolate	Sweet and savory snacks made using non-permitted flours, licorice
Drinks	Wine, liquor, liqueurs, cider; tea, pure coffee, cocoa, carbonated drinks, juices, most concentrates and soft drinks	Real ales, beer, lager, stout; coffee or other drinks containing barley, malted drinks, vending-machine drinks
Miscellaneous	Pure salt, pepper, herbs, spices, vinegar, baking soda, cream of tartar; curry powder, baking powder, yeast, extracts, dressings, honey, jellies, molasses, marmalade, nut butters	Spices, baking powders, dressings or any other ingredients containing wheat, rye, barley, or uncontaminated oats; some medicines and vitamins; spreads containing wheat flour

Gluten-free foods

Moderate amounts of oats may be suitable for some people with celiac disease—check with your doctor.

Not all alcoholic drinks are gluten-free, so check gluten-free guides.

To help make gluten-free diets more varied, specially manufactured gluten-free products have been developed. These include bread, cookies, cakes, flour mixes, breakfast cereals, and pasta.

You may see products described as either "wheat starch/gluten-free" or "wheat-free/gluten-free." This is because "wheat starch/gluten-free" products are based on wheat starch that has gluten removed to a level that will not cause damage to the intestine. Unlike "wheat-free/gluten-free" products, they are not suitable for wheat-free diets, but both types are suitable for people suffering from celiac disease.

FREQUENTLY ASKED QUESTIONS

It is vital to go shopping with official gluten-free food guides from national celiac societies, to look for gluten-free symbols and, when in doubt, to leave it out.

WHAT ABOUT OATS?

Oats contain proteins similar to gliadin, but in much smaller amounts than wheat, barley, and rye. Research has shown that most people with celiac disease can safely eat moderate amounts of pure uncontaminated oats (some oats may be contaminated with gluten from wheat products). But, as some people react much more strongly to gluten than others, the safest approach is to assume that oats are off your menu.

WHAT ABOUT DRUGS, MEDICINES, OR SUPPLEMENTS?

It is possible that these contain gluten in some form, so it is wise to check with your doctor and/or pharmacist before taking prescriptions or over-the-counter medications. In the case of supplements, you may need to contact the manufacturer.

WHAT ABOUT POSTAGE STAMPS?

As a general rule, the gum used on postage stamps is gluten-free, alternatively use self-adhesive stamps.

WHAT ABOUT KIDS' PAINTS, GLUE, & PLAY DOUGH?

These are not always gluten-free, look for alternatives and ensure children with celiac disease don't put them in their mouths.

CAN I EAT MALT AND MALT EXTRACT?

Barley malt and barley flour should be avoided. However barley malt extract is generally at a much lower level but some malted breakfast cereals are not suitable for celiacs.

WHICH ALCOHOLIC DRINKS ARE SUITABLE?

Gluten-free drinks include all wines, champagnes, ciders, perries, liquor (including malt whiskey), liqueurs, ports, vermouths, and sherries. Avoid all beers, lagers, real ales, and stouts.

WHAT ABOUT MODIFIED STARCH AND MALTODEXTRIN ?

Modified starch could be gluten-free if the starch comes from potato, corn, rice, or tapioca. However, it could be made from wheat, barley, or rye. Maltodextrin is gluten-free.

IS IT OKAY TO TOUCH GLUTEN-CONTAINING PRODUCTS?

This will not cause an adverse reaction as gluten is only a problem if it is actually eaten or breathed in.

Specially-manufactured gluten-free foods help make a gluten-free diet more varied.

Choosing a balanced diet

Enjoying a balanced diet is important for everyone, including people following a gluten-free diet. A balanced diet should include a selection from all of the five food groups listed in the table that follows. This is only a general guide and is not meant for children under five, who have different dietary needs (see pages 24–25). To ensure that the processed foods you choose are gluten-free, read all labels carefully and/or check to see if they are listed in official gluten-free food directories from national celiac societies.

	Main nutrients	What to choose	How much
Potatoes, rice, gluten-free breads, cereals, pasta, and other grains 	Carbohydrate • fiber • B vitamins • potassium • some protein • iron • vitamin E • calcium • phytochemicals*	Rice • potatoes • yams • gluten-free bread and crackers, rice and corn cakes • gluten-free pasta, noodles, breakfast cereals • other gluten-free grains	5–11 portions daily One portion: 1 slice of bread 1 bowl of cereal 3 crispbreads 3½ oz cooked rice, pasta, or noodles
Fruit and vegetables	Vitamin C • folic acid • beta-carotene • fiber • magnesium • potassium • some carbohydrate • iron • calcium • phytochemicals*	All types: fresh, frozen, canned, dried • juices	5–9 portions daily One portion: a medium fruit 2–3 tablespoons vegetables glass of juice 1 tablespoon dried fruit

	Main nutrients	What to choose	How much
Milk and dairy foods, and alternatives 	Calcium • protein • vitamins B2, B12, A, and D • zinc • phytochemicals* in soy-based foods	Lower-fat varieties such as reduced-fat milks, yogurt, and cheeses • calcium-fortified soy milk or yogurt	2–3 portions daily One portion: ³/₄ cup milk small carton yogurt 1 oz cheese ½ cup cottage cheese
Meat, fish, and alternatives 	Protein • iron • B vitamins • zinc • magnesium • potassium • phytochemicals* in peas, beans, lentils, nuts, seeds, tofu	Lean and trimmed meats • poultry • fish • eggs • beans • split peas • lentils • nuts • meat substitutes	2–3 portions daily One portion: 3½ oz meat 5 oz fish 1–2 eggs 4–5 tablespoons cooked beans
Foods rich in fat and/or sugar 	Fat, including some essential fats • vitamins • minerals and sugars • phytochemicals* in virgin olive oil, sesame oil, and chocolate	Unsaturated oils such as olive, canola, peanut, soy, and their spreads • lower-fat dressings and ready meals • nuts are a good choice for snacks	Eat in small amounts, especially foods high in saturated fat. Check labels carefully to ensure products are gluten-free.

* Phytochemicals are natural compounds found in fruit, vegetables, legumes, brown rice, buckwheat, millet, nuts, and seeds. They give plants their distinct taste, texture, and colors. They are not true nutrients but seem to protect our health in different ways. Some block the development of cancer cells, others influence chemical reactions that regulate body functions and many work as antioxidants—this why greens are so good for us!

Salt, alcohol, and fluid

SALT

Everybody needs a little salt, but it is important to watch your intake, especially if you suffer from high blood pressure. A liking for salt is very much down to habit and if you cut down gradually your tastebuds will adjust. Try these tips to help you keep to the recommended limit of 6 g (around 1 teaspoon) a day.

- Around three-quarters of the salt we eat comes from processed foods, so cook with fresh ingredients whenever possible.
- Look out for salt-reduced canned and packaged foods.
- Limit or skip adding salt when cooking or at the table.
- Use herbs, spices, garlic, wine, lemon juice, vinegar, and tomato paste to add natural flavor to cooking.
- Salt usually appears as sodium chloride on food labels. To convert to grams of salt, multiply the sodium value by 2.5. So, for example, 2.2 g sodium will give you 5.5 g salt.

ALCOHOL

Most of us enjoy a drink but keep in mind "sensible" limits. The US Department of Health and Human Services recommends that men do not regularly exceed 2 drinks a day and women 1 drink a day. The guidelines define 1 drink as:

- a 5 ounce glass of wine or champagne
- 1.5 ounces of 80-proof distilled spirits
- a 3 ounce glass of sherry or port.

All of these drinks are suitable on a gluten-free diet.

DRINK ENOUGH FLUID

Around two-thirds of the body is made up of fluid. This is constantly lost when we sweat and breathe, as well as in urine and bowel motions. To replace these losses most people need to drink at least 6 cups of fluid each day. More is needed in hot weather and/or if you are exercising. To check that you are drinking enough, note the color of your urine. It should be a light straw color; if it is dark, then you need to drink more.

It is important to drink plenty of fluids daily.

Healthy gluten-free cooking

REFRIGERATOR AND PANTRY ESSENTIALS

Stock your refrigerator with fish, chicken, eggs, lean meat, a range of dairy foods, fruit, and fresh or frozen vegetables. Also make sure that you have a variety of gluten-free basics in your pantry ready for quick, nutritious meal and snack preparation (always double-check branded processed foods with your official gluten-free food guide). Take time to experiment with new ingredients and gluten-free grains, and to adapt favorite recipes. Most ingredients can be bought from supermarkets but visit health food stores and specialty internet sites too if you want to try more exotic items.

ESSENTIAL PANTRY ITEMS
- Canned or dried beans, peas, lentils
- Gluten-free breakfast cereals, millet flakes
- Corn crispbread, rice cakes
- Canned salmon, mackerel, sardines, tuna
- Rice, corn, and gluten-free pasta and noodles
- Buckwheat, millet, tapioca, sago
- Canned tomatoes, passata (sieved tomatoes), corn, new potatoes
- Popping corn, plain nuts, seeds
- Dried apricots, figs, raisins
- Canned tropical fruit and berries
- Lemon and lime juice, salad dressings, flavored vinegars, garlic, onion, ginger, chili, other herbs and spices, soy sauce, hot sauce, capers, olives, wine, tomato paste, mustard—make sure these are gluten-free
- Olive, canola, sesame, walnut, or chili oil

COOKING TIP

Xanthan gum is gluten-free and becomes "stretchy" when wet which makes bread, cakes, and pastry softer, with a less crumbly texture. Mix in 1 teaspoon of xanthan gum per cup of gluten-free flour before adding wet ingredients as per your recipe.

Healthy cooking equipment
- Steamer
- Nonstick pans
- Barbecue
- Wok
- Food processor
- Pressure cooker
- Skillet
- Oil spray
- Natural bristle brush
- Vegetable scrubber and peeler

Stock your pantry with healthy gluten-free ingredients, such as dried fruit snacks.

Gluten-free eating for different ages

BABIES AND YOUNG CHILDREN

If babies or toddlers are going to develop celiac disease, it usually happens between the ages of nine months and three years. Both breast milk and infant formula are gluten-free, so a baby's predisposition to celiac disease will not appear until weaning starts. All mothers—including those with celiac disease—are encouraged to breast-feed for at least six months and to start weaning from six months of age. If parents choose to start weaning before this, it is advised not to start before four months of age, and then with gluten-free foods. This is especially important if celiac disease runs in the family. If your baby is healthy, gluten-containing foods such as wheat-based cereals, bread, and pasta can be gradually introduced from six months, as part of a normal infant's diet. Since your baby will be stronger at this age, if he or she is going to develop celiac disease it is best to let it happen clearly, to allow for easier diagnosis (see page 9). Once diagnosed, all sources of gluten must be strictly excluded from the diet.

Parents are encouraged to start weaning from six months of age.

Expert dietary advice from a dietitian is essential to ensure that your baby gets the nutrition necessary for growth and development. Once the gluten-free diet starts, he or she will gradually return to being a happy, healthy child. Regular checkups with the doctor and dietitian are essential. It can also be helpful to meet with other parents who have young children with celiac disease to share experiences and support.

SCHOOL-AGE CHILDREN

Once children get close to school age they will be aware that there is something different about them, so it is best to talk openly and positively about their celiac disease and gluten-free diet, both to them and to others. Educating your child (and any carers) about a gluten-free diet is vital too, so he or she will be able to manage at school, birthday parties, or any meal away from home. Schools should be able to provide gluten-free meals, but if not, a packed lunch is the best option.

Children use a lot of energy—they are growing and developing, they rush around playing—so they need nourishing food for fuel. Early experience of food will also help shape their eating habits in later life. By continuing to be a good role model, parents can encourage children to enjoy and experience a wide variety of tasty and nourishing gluten-free foods, as well as help them to understand why their diet is different. Relaxed family meals away from the television and other distractions, and with shared gluten-free dishes, helps to develop the social side and positive pleasures of food too.

Make sure you and your child see the dietitian regularly for individualized advice about nutritional needs. If your child was very unwell before diagnosis, he or she may struggle to enjoy food at all. Regular contact helps to ensure that the diet is strictly followed and can also reassure parents that they are right not to give their children gluten-containing "treats"—which are no doubt asked for.

Make sure your child's specific dietary needs are catered for at any events away from home, such as friends' birthday parties.

Feeding young children with celiac disease

- Three family-type gluten-free meals, plus snacks such as gluten-free toast, yogurt, fruit, vegetable sticks, fruit shakes, to suit appetite
- Two or three servings of calcium-rich foods such as whole milk, follow-on milk, gluten-free cheese sauce, yogurt, cheese
- Vitamin D from food and some gentle sunlight (see page 30)
- Iron and vitamin C-rich foods (see page 29)
- If children are away from home, make sure carers understand the gluten-free diet

Packed lunches are the best option if a gluten-free lunch at school can't be ensured.

TEENAGE YEARS

Around 95 percent of the maximum strength of the skeleton is laid down by late teens. More protein, calcium, and zinc are needed to help build new tissue, muscle, and bone, and menstruation means girls' iron requirements almost double. Meanwhile, busy social lives can lead to skipped meals or convenience food. Body-image concerns are common, as is experimentation with food fads.

Having to follow a gluten-free diet on top of all this can make things tricky. Teenagers are likely to need extra help and advice about eating out safely and choosing suitable alcoholic drinks. Hungry boys, in particular, need plenty of gluten-free snacks to reduce the chance of dietary lapses. Following the diet strictly ensures that nutrients are absorbed properly, thus enabling increased nutritional needs to be met. It also helps teenagers to feel well and so reduces the risk of low moods—which can be enough of a problem at that age.

The main thing is for parents and their children to maintain a sense of proportion. While a strict gluten-free diet is very important, the occasional lapse will not ruin everything. Accepting this fact will help everyone.

PREGNANCY

Nutrition affects every aspect of our bodily functions, including fertility and pregnancy. A baby develops rapidly during the first six to eight weeks, and women may not realize they are pregnant for a lot of this time. This means it is important for women, and men too, to be well nourished before they start trying for a baby. Sadly, untreated celiac disease in either partner increases the risk of infertility or miscarriage, but people with well-managed celiac disease can look forward to a healthy pregnancy.

It is recommended that all women planning pregnancy (and then for the first 12 weeks of pregnancy) should take a daily 400 microgram folic acid supplement to reduce the risk of neural tube defects such as spina bifida. Eating more foods rich in folic acid is also advisable (see page 20), and research suggests that good intakes of all B vitamins, zinc, magnesium, and calcium are important for the baby's health.

If you have recently been diagnosed with celiac disease or are not confident that your diet is well balanced, it makes sense to take a multivitamin and mineral supplement. However, make sure its nutrients do not exceed the recommended daily amounts, as high doses of some nutrients, such as vitamin A, may adversely affect the healthy growth and development of the baby (it is important to note that liver is very high in vitamin A, so it must be avoided during pregnancy). Supplements designed for pregnancy are a good choice, but if you are unsure speak to your doctor, dietitian, or pharmacist.

A BALANCED DIET

At your first antenatal check, normally with your doctor or midwife, make sure the relevant people know you have celiac disease. Pregnancy does not literally mean having to "eat for two" (you need to increase your calorie intake by just 200 a day, and then only in the last three months), but the quality of your diet is important. Keeping strictly to your balanced gluten-free diet will optimize nutrient absorption and minimize any risk of problems such as anemia.

Foods rich in omega-3 fats—oily fish, walnuts, canola oil, pumpkin seeds, and omega-3 enriched eggs—are important for the baby's developing brain, retina, and nervous system. Vitamin D is needed to absorb and use calcium properly, so supplements may be advised for pregnant and breast-feeding women with limited exposure to sunlight.

BREAST-FEEDING

Breast milk provides the optimal balance of nutrients for growth and development, as well as antibodies to build up immunity. Infant formula, which contains all the additional, essential nutrients, is available for mothers who are unable or choose not to breast-feed. The mother's nutrient needs increase more during breast-feeding than pregnancy, especially for calcium, magnesium, zinc, and vitamin C (see page 21). On average, breast-feeding women need an extra 500 calories a day, so this can be wisely "spent" on extra low-fat dairy foods, fish, fruit, and vegetables.

Foods rich in omega-3 fats, such as oily fish and walnuts, are important during pregnancy.

ELDERLY PEOPLE

Celiac disease can arrive at any time of life. About 20 percent of people diagnosed with the condition are over 60 and some are even over 80. If people have other health problems or just feel that they are suffering from "old age," the danger is that their symptoms will be overlooked.

Good nutrition is vital throughout life to keep the immune system strong and to maintain health and well-being. With increasing age, calorie needs usually decline, but some vitamin and mineral needs increase as the body uses or absorbs them less efficiently. Real problems can start if people are not following their gluten-free diet properly or interest in food wanes because of poor appetite, a limited budget, loneliness, illness, or medication. A once-a-day multivitamin and mineral supplement is prudent for people over 65, while a weekly check on weight will flag up unhealthy weight loss, which is a sign that extra medical and nutritional help may be needed.

Celiac disease affects people of all ages and good nutrition is important throughout life.

Anemia

The symptoms of anemia include tiredness, feeling irritable, lack of appetite, lower resistance to infection, and breathlessness. In children, it can also affect their development, concentration, and performance at school.

If you are anemic, when diagnosed your doctor may prescribe supplements, and your dietitian will advise on how to include iron-rich foods in your gluten-free diet. Strictly following your gluten-free diet is vital, as it allows your body to absorb iron and other nutrients properly.

Preventing anemia

- Good sources of iron include liver, red meat, oily fish, shellfish, beans and lentils, iron-fortified gluten-free breakfast cereals, poultry, green vegetables, nuts, dried fruit, and gluten-free bread.
- The iron found in foods of animal origin is absorbed much better than iron from non-meat sources such as pulses, gluten-free cereals, nuts, and green vegetables.
- Vitamin C-rich fruit, vegetables, or juices with meals boosts iron absorption from non-meat foods. This is especially important for vegetarians (see page 34).
- Coffee and especially tea can reduce iron absorption. Teenage girls and women of child-bearing age, who are at higher risk of iron deficiency, should aim to drink tea between rather than with meals.

BABIES' IRON REQUIREMENTS

By six months of age, babies' natural iron stores have run out, so they need iron-rich foods in their daily diet: for example, red meat and iron-fortified gluten-free baby cereals or legumes of a suitable consistency, prepared without added salt or sugar. Breast milk or infant formula—around 2½ cups per day—should be their main drink until babies are a year old. Whole cows' milk can then be introduced as part of their balanced diet.

Vitamin C-rich foods and juices help the body absorb iron from non-meat foods.

Calcium and bone health

Bones are made up of a network of fibers packed with bone crystals. These crystals are rich in calcium and other minerals that give bones their strength and "density." Osteoporosis develops when bones have lost so much of their mineral content that they become brittle and break easily. People with celiac disease must take special care to protect themselves from osteoporosis, because they may not absorb calcium and other nutrients as well as they should. Studies suggest that up to 50 percent of people with celiac disease may have low bone density. Fortunately, research shows that once children are on a gluten-free diet, bone density improves.

As we have already seen, most of our bone strength is achieved by late teens. However, bones continue to develop until the age of about 25, and from 35 they gradually thin. Hormonal changes at the menopause also increase bone density loss in women. In addition to celiac disease, too little calcium when young, inactivity, smoking, corticosteroid drugs for asthma, early menopause, eating disorders, and a family history of the condition increase the risk of osteoporosis. Talk to your doctor if any of these apply to you. If necessary, you can have a bone scan to assess your bone density.

FEED YOUR BONES

- Enjoy a balanced diet, as a wide range of nutrients—not just calcium—is needed for healthy bones.
- Get enough calcium: choose two or three servings of dairy foods daily (low-fat types are still rich in calcium), plus other good sources such as greens, legumes, fortified gluten-free bread, and canned fish with bones (see opposite). Your doctor or dietitian may also advise a supplement.
- Get enough vitamin D, which controls calcium absorption. Most comes from the action of gentle sunlight on the skin. Food sources include oily fish, eggs, cheese, and fortified foods such

Dairy foods are an important source of bone-building calcium.

as gluten-free cereals and margarine. Daily supplements (no more than 10 micrograms) may be advisable for people over 65, women who are pregnant during the winter, those whose skin is always covered, and house-bound people.

- Eat at least five portions of fruit and vegetables daily (see page 20). Diets high in the minerals potassium and magnesium, from fruit and vegetables, are linked to stronger bones in later life.
- If you smoke, aim to stop. Keep to sensible drinking limits (see page 22).
- Note that many specially manufactured gluten-free products are fortified with calcium and contain higher levels than their gluten-containing versions.

EXERCISE YOUR BONES

- Stay active with weekly weight-bearing exercise: for example, brisk walking, aerobics, skipping, dancing, and resistance training to put stress on bones.
- Just move more often. Regular activity improves balance, coordination, flexibility, and muscle strength, which in turn help to reduce the risk of falling and breaking a bone.

Regular exercise puts stress on bones, helping to keep them strong.

Weight control

Weight loss is a common symptom of untreated celiac disease. Once they start their gluten-free diet, however, most people gradually regain the lost weight. If you find that this does not happen, then contact your dietitian. It may be that you are unwittingly eating gluten, or simply that you would benefit from some healthy, calorie-boosting additions to your diet. Children should see their doctor and dietitian regularly to ensure that their weight, height, and general development are progressing normally.

WATCHING YOUR WEIGHT

Being overweight rather than underweight is more common for people with treated celiac disease. No doubt this is at least in part the result of feeling well and enjoying food once your condition has been diagnosed. It is also not surprising when you consider that over half of all adults are overweight. Being overweight can affect health in many ways. It increases the risk of Type 2 diabetes, heart disease, high blood pressure, back and joint pain, infertility, and certain cancers, so it is not just a cosmetic issue.

The calories we consume (food and drink) and the calories we burn (metabolism and activity) largely determine body weight. To keep weight stable these must be in balance and to lose weight you must take in fewer calories than you burn. These days most people in the West need to take care to eat wisely and stay active as we are all being constantly beset by tempting food at a time when labor-saving devices mean less and less energy-expending activity is needed.

To lose weight at a healthy rate of around 1 pound a week you need to eat 500 fewer calories than you usually do every day. To do this you do not have to change your diet radically or count calories all the time. Some simple lifestyle changes, taken step by step, can tip the balance in your favor. For example, switching to lower-fat foods and cooking methods, swapping some high-fat snacks for fruit, and building in extra daily activity (see opposite) could be enough.

Try to choose healthy snacks, such as fruit, instead of ones which are high in fat or sugar.

Successful slimmers swear by these tips:

- Be realistic about target weights and rate of weight loss.
- Think long-term rather than following rigid or quick-fix diet plans.
- Keep a food and thoughts diary to identify problem areas—you will stay aware of what and why you eat, make conscious food choices, and identify comfort eating or negative thoughts.
- Plan ahead for regular meals and snacks.
- Include at least five portions of fruit and vegetables in your diet every day (see page 20).
- Eat lower-fat foods and use low-fat cooking methods (see right).
- Avoid rigid rules that can lead to "all or nothing" thinking: for example, "I have failed by eating that chocolate so I might as well keep on eating."
- Make a list of distractions—such as going for a walk or taking a bath—to use when cravings strike. If you do succumb, put it behind you and plan how to deal with the situation next time.
- Enlist support from a health professional, friend, or partner.

STAY ACTIVE

Being active not only helps you to stay in shape but also decreases your risk of heart disease, contributes to mood and stress management, and is good for your bones. All types of physical activity are beneficial. Here are some ideas:

- Use the stairs instead of the lift at work.
- Get off the bus a stop earlier and walk the rest of the way.
- Use the toilet on the next floor up at work.
- Walk or cycle short distances rather than jumping into the car.
- Spend less time sitting or watching TV.
- Build up to 30 minutes (or two 15-minute sessions) of moderate activity at least five times a week. Choose something you enjoy and incorporate it into your daily routine, for example: cycling, a lunchtime walk, dancing, aerobics, martial arts, gardening.
- Add a brisk 30-minute walk to your daily routine and you could lose 12 lb of fat in a year.

If you are very overweight or have a medical problem, consult your doctor before you make changes to your activity levels.

Healthy cooking tips
- Buy lean meat or trim off any excess fat.
- Broil, bake, microwave, steam, poach, stir-fry, or casserole foods instead of frying them. Oil sprays are useful. Roast meat on a rack to allow the fat to drain off.
- Serve baked, mashed, boiled, or new potatoes. Oven fries and chunky wedges are better choices than deep-fried French fries.
- Low-fat fromage frais and yogurts make tasty alternatives to cream, sour cream, or mayonnaise.
- Try using tomato paste, garlic, herbs, spices, olives, vinegar, lemon juice, wine, or hot pepper sauces rather than extra fat to flavor food.

Baked potatoes are a much healthier choice than fried and can be served with a variety of toppings.

Vegetarian diets

People choose to become vegetarian for a variety of reasons and a well-balanced vegetarian diet can be health-promoting and enjoyable. However, it is another food restriction on top of the gluten-free diet, so extra care is needed, particularly for those with special nutritional needs: for example, children and teenagers, and pregnant and breast-feeding women. You should see a dietitian for the best information about vegetarian diets. This is even more important if you choose to follow a vegan diet, which excludes all animal products, including eggs and dairy foods.

A QUESTION OF BALANCE

When you exclude meat and fish, nutritious alternatives are needed to replace the protein, iron, zinc, and B vitamins found in these foods. Legumes (peas, beans, and lentils), eggs, tofu, TVP, nuts, and seeds are all suitable and are naturally gluten-free.

Legumes are a nutritious alternative to meat in a vegetarian diet.

Milk and dairy foods are important too, but they are from a separate food group (see page 20) and lack iron, so it is not enough to cut out meat and replace it with cheese. If people eat few or no dairy foods, soy milk fortified with calcium and vitamin B12 (B12 is found naturally only in foods of animal origin) should be used daily, along with other calcium-rich foods (see page 30). Dairy foods are also important sources of iodine, which is needed for healthy functioning of the thyroid gland. Other good vegetarian sources are seaweed, iodized salt, and fortified yeast extracts.

Brazil nuts are a rich source of the mineral selenium which can be low in a vegetarian diet.

Gluten-free breads, pastas, and cereals, potatoes, rice, and other gluten-free grains provide a healthy, filling basis for vegetarian meals and are reasonable iron providers. Standard wholegrain cereals add the mineral selenium to the diet and this may give protection against many long-term diseases, and also regulate mood. Good gluten-free sources include nuts, especially brazil nuts, sunflower seeds, and dairy foods. Fish is a rich source too, but is off the menu for vegetarians. Fruit and vegetables are also naturally gluten-free and provide vital vitamin C, which boosts iron absorption from non-meat foods.

Diabetes

Out of every 25 people with Type 1 (insulin-dependent) diabetes, one will also have celiac disease, because of a genetic link between the two conditions. People with Type 1 diabetes have a greater chance of developing celiac disease (and vice versa) than the general population. Many experts recommend that everyone with Type 1 diabetes be tested for celiac disease (see page 11), especially those with bowel problems or unexplained anemia.

Type 1 diabetes usually affects people under 40 and is a lifelong condition. People with untreated Type 1 diabetes have too much sugar (glucose) in the blood because their body stops producing insulin, a hormone that regulates blood glucose levels. The main symptoms of untreated diabetes are thirst, frequent trips to the toilet, extreme tiredness, weight loss, and blurred vision.

Type 1 diabetes is treated with insulin injections, a healthy diet, and regular activity. Appropriate treatment reduces the risk of long-term complications such as heart disease and eye, kidney, and nerve problems. Your diabetes team will give you personal advice about all of these, but here are some general pointers:

- Eat regular meals and snacks based on starchy foods such as rice, potatoes, legumes, gluten-free bread, cereals, pasta, and crackers, fruit, or yogurt.
- Aim for at least five portions of fruit, vegetables, and legumes each day (see page 20). They are brimming with vitamins and fiber, as well as protective antioxidants, which help to keep the circulation healthy.
- Cut down on fat, especially saturated fat, which can raise cholesterol levels. This is found in fatty meats, full-fat dairy foods, butter, cream, and gluten-free cakes and cookies.
- Limit sugar, especially sugary drinks, since too much can raise blood glucose too quickly, making levels difficult to control.
- Keep to sensible salt and alcohol limits (see page 22).
- Enjoy one portion of oily fish such as canned salmon, sardines, mackerel, pilchards, or trout each week. They provide omega-3 fats, which are especially good for heart health.

People with diabetes are advised to have regular meals and snacks based on starchy foods.

Lactose intolerance

Lactose is a natural sugar found only in milk. Normally it is broken down by the digestive enzyme lactase and absorbed into the body. If lactase levels are too low, the lactose remains undigested and passes into the large intestine, where it attracts water. Meanwhile, natural bacteria in the bowel ferment the undigested lactose, causing wind, bloating, and watery diarrhea.

LACTOSE INTOLERANCE AND CELIAC DISEASE

Lactose intolerance can be a long-term genetic condition or a temporary problem brought on by a bad attack of gastroenteritis or a flare-up of a health problem that affects the bowel, such as untreated celiac disease. Once a strict gluten-free diet is started, the lactose intolerance usually resolves itself. For some, however, it remains a chronic problem.

Lactose intolerance is best diagnosed via a controlled food challenge (see page 11). Your doctor may also arrange for a "breath hydrogen test." People with celiac disease are at higher risk of osteoporosis, so they need to ensure a good calcium intake (see page 30). Dairy foods are the richest sources, so if you cannot tolerate them alternatives are vital. You may find you can manage some dairy foods (see left), but if not, be sure to use other rich sources, such as calcium-fortified soy milk and orange juice, daily.

MANAGING LACTOSE INTOLERANCE

Most people with lactose intolerance can manage some lactose in their diet: for example, up to a glass of milk spread over the day. Research also suggests that lactose intolerance can be improved by gradually increasing the amount of lactose included in the diet, since bacteria in the large intestine seem to adapt to break down lactose.

Dairy products with a low lactose content such as hard cheese, butter, and bio-yogurts are usually quite well tolerated. Some trial and error will be involved to find what levels suit you. If you are at all unsure, talk to your dietitian about it first.

Foods containing lactose
- Milk—all types
- Goats' and sheep's milk
- Milk powder, milk solids
- Buttermilk
- Cheese, cheese powder, cheese flavor
- Yogurt, live yogurt
- Fromage frais
- Butter, margarine (unless it's milk-free)
- Cream/ artificial cream
- Ice cream
- Milk sugar
- Milk chocolate
- Lactose
- Hydrolyzed casein
- Whey/whey protein/whey syrup sweetener

Bowel problems

A gluten-free diet means that many cereal foods and wholegrains are no longer on the menu. Since these are important sources of bowel-regulating fiber, many people find that constipation can be a problem. On the other hand, for some people, their bowels remain a bit grumbly and loose after starting a gluten-free diet. If you suffer from either problem, check out these general guidelines. If your problems persist, speak to your doctor and/or dietitian.

CONSTIPATION

Increase the fiber content of your diet and make sure you are drinking enough fluid, because fiber needs fluid to bulk up and work properly. Regular exercise and leaving enough time in the morning—or whenever—for a relaxed sit on the toilet also help deal with the problem.

How to boost your fiber intake

- Have regular meals, starting with breakfast.
- Opt for brown rice and potatoes with skins.
- Include at least five portions of fruit and vegetables in your daily diet—fresh, canned, frozen, and juiced (see page 20).
- Include baked beans, other beans, lentils, and peas regularly in soups, stews, as a vegetable, in salads, or as a snack on toast.
- Different nuts and seeds make high-fiber snacks or additions to salads and rice dishes.
- Choose higher-fiber varieties of specially manufactured gluten-free foods.
- Drink at least 6 cups of fluid each day (see page 22).
- Try bio-yogurts or drinks which contain "live" lactobacillus bacteria regularly (this may help loose bowels as well as constipation).
- Make changes slowly to let your bowel adapt and so avoid excess flatulence.

Starting the day with a high-fiber breakfast helps to keep the bowels in good working order.

Menu plans

These menu plans suggest ways to include the recipes in this book in your gluten-free diet. They show just how varied and tasty meals can be for you and the whole family, and also give ideas for meals if you are following additional dietary regimes: for example, a vegetarian or lactose-free diet.

	Breakfast	Lunch	Evening meal	Snacks
Standard gluten-free	Breakfast cereal bars Banana	Toasted open sandwich Fruit yogurt	Fish cakes with fennel mayonnaise Green leaf salad Caramel fruit pudding	Fresh fruit Lemony polenta cake
	Potato drop scones Glass of apple juice	Walnut, pear, & green leaf salad Gluten-free crackers Fresh fruit	Loin of pork with lentils, with new potatoes Cherry & almond clafoutis	Fruited teacake Fresh fruit
Vegetarian, gluten-free	Breakfast cornbread with eggs Glass of orange juice	Lentil & rosemary soup, with Homemade bread	Roasted vegetable & red bean stew with rice Sweet pancakes with citrus sauce	Dried fruit and nuts Yogurt
	Cranberry, banana, & sesame smoothie	Hummus with crudites and Spicy bread	Mushroom risotto with salad Pannacotta with blueberry sauce	Fresh fruit Lemony glazed shortbread
Lactose-free, gluten-free	Millet, fruit, & nut granola with soy milk and banana	Chili rice noodles Fresh fruit	Mediterranean lamb casserole Summer pudding	Soy yogurt Fresh fruit
	Mango, orange, & soy milkshake	Potato & onion tortilla, with salad Fruited teacake	Thai coconut chicken, with jasmine rice Sorbet, fresh mango	Almond macaroons Fresh fruit
Diabetes, gluten-free	Homemade bread with favorite spread Glass of orange juice	Chicken & ham soup Salad Fresh fruit	Spiced beef with spinach, with basmati rice Fruited teacake	Fresh fruit Fruit yogurt
	Spiced apple porridge Glass of apple juice	Chickpea flatbread Fruit yogurt	Baked trout with pine nuts, with new potatoes and salad Almond macaroons	Rice cakes Fresh fruit

	Breakfast	Lunch	Evening meal	Snacks
Young children	Spiced apple porridge Diluted fruit juice	Cheese on gluten-free bread Fruit yogurt	Little cottage pies Favorite vegetables Plain cupcake	Banana Glass of milk
	Crisped rice cereal with milk Diluted fruit juice	Parsnip & fresh ginger soup Potato drop scones	Homemade veggie sausage & beans Sliced fruit	Fruit yogurt Glass of milk
School-age children	Cornflakes with milk Gluten-free toast with peanut butter Glass of juice	Gluten-free sandwiches Packet of plain chips Fresh fruit	Potato pizza margherita Salad Rainbow popsicles	Corn & bacon muffin Fruit yogurt
	Spiced apple porridge Glass of juice	Filled baked potato Fruited teacake	Sticky chicken drumsticks Oven fries, peas, carrots Fruit yogurt	Breakfast cereal bars Mango, orange, & soy milkshake

IDEAS FOR ENTERTAINING

Spiced and salted nuts for a predinner nibble. Spicy fruit and seed bread to serve with dinner

Appetizers

Prosciutto with melon

Millet "tabbouleh"

Chilled gazpacho

Mascarpone, feta, & herb pâté—serve with crudites and gluten-free toast

Toasted open sandwiches

Walnut, pear, & green leaf salad

Buckwheat blinis with smoked fish

Parsnip & fresh ginger soup

Main Courses

(serve with potatoes or rice, vegetables or salad)

Summer roast chicken

Thai coconut chicken

Baked trout with pine nuts

Loin of pork with lentils

Mediterranean lamb casserole

Roasted vegetable & red bean stew

Mushroom risotto made with wild mushrooms

Chili rice noodles

Desserts

Strawberry meringue roulade

Apricot & marzipan tart

Caramel fruit pudding

Fruit salad, served with (gluten-free) vanilla ice cream

Cherry & almond clafoutis

Coffee & almond trifle

Pannacotta with blueberry sauce

Eating away from home

You cannot afford to leave eating out to chance. Think carefully about what friends, hotels, or restaurants might serve, and what food will be available when you are traveling or out for a busy day. Before long, planning, questioning, and bringing along gluten-free foods will become second nature. Catering processes can limit safe choices unless you know the restaurant or bar well. Use these guidelines to help you through the maze:

Italian

- Pasta, bruschetta, minestrone, garlic bread, cheese sauces, and fried fish are off the menu.
- Seafood salad, tomato, avocado, and mozzarella salad, or melon and prosciutto make good starters.
- Chicken, fish, or liver cooked in sauces without flour are the best main-course options.

Chinese

- Avoid soy sauce.
- Skip starters unless you can be sure they are not battered, crumbed, or thickened with flour.
- Ask for non-thickened stir-fried dishes made without soy sauce and served with rice.

Indian

- Tikka and tandoori dishes with no sauce, served with salad and rice, are the safest options.
- Most curries are made with catering-pack sauces which may contain wheat flour. Order only where you can be certain no wheat flour has been used.
- Avoid any breads on the menu.

Burger restaurants

- Most burger chains have comprehensive ingredients lists for their products, so ask for a copy.
- Bring your own gluten-free burger bun.

Children's party ideas

Mini gluten-free sandwiches (check all ingredients are gluten-free):

- Savory fillings: cold meat, roast chicken, cheese spread, tuna, egg, hummus, peanut butter, yeast extract.
- Sweet fillings: banana and honey, jelly, dates, sliced strawberries and cream cheese.

Mini Potato pizza margheritas

Corn and bacon muffins, cut into quarters

Potato and onion tortilla, cut into cubes

Hummus

Vegetable sticks—sliced peppers, carrots, mushrooms, and celery

Cubes of cheese

Sticky chicken drumsticks (better for older children)

Homemade veggie sausages & beans

Baked potatoes

Plain chips

Fresh fruit—cut into chunks

Fruited teacake

Almond macaroons

Rainbow popsicles

Chocolate lover's birthday cake

Flower cupcakes

Chocolate fudge crisps

Water, diluted juice, and well-diluted concentrate to drink

Checklist
- Always check that food or drink is gluten-free.
- Take gluten-free foods/snacks with you.
- Check that workplaces serve gluten-free meals or provide facilities for storing or preparing your own.
- Remember to tell anyone who is cooking for you that you can't eat gluten.
- Check in advance that a restaurant can confidently provide gluten-free meals (ask them to check ready-prepared food with the catering supplier).
- Check that the meal you want to order is gluten-free—if there is any doubt, do not order it.
- Plan ahead for snacks for a long train, car, or plane journey.
- Find out what foods are available in vacation destinations and hotels.

GETTING FURTHER HELP AND INFORMATION

Following a restricted diet of any type can be tricky, and sometimes isolating, especially when it is a lifelong commitment. Sharing knowledge and experiences, and just being able to chat to people who either live with or know about the condition, can be a great help and support. This is equally true for children of all ages as well as adults.

National and local charities and support groups exist in most countries, so find your nearest group and make the most of what it has to offer.

Potato drop scones

Makes 12 • **Preparation:** 10 minutes • **Cooking:** 20–25 minutes

1 lb 2 oz large potatoes

1½ teaspoons Gluten-free
  baking powder (see below)

2 medium eggs

5 tablespoons whole milk

salt and pepper

oil for frying

GLUTEN-FREE BAKING POWDER

¾ cup rice flour

3 tablespoons baking soda

3 tablespoons tartaric acid

Preparation: 5–10 minutes

Mix together all the
ingredients and sift several
times. Store the powder in a
screw-top jar.

1 Cut the potatoes into small chunks and cook in boiling, lightly salted water for 15 minutes or until completely tender. Drain well, return to the pan, and mash until smooth. Allow to cool slightly.

2 Beat in the baking powder, then the eggs, milk, and a little seasoning, and continue to beat until everything is evenly combined.

3 Heat a little oil in a heavy skillet. Drop heaping dessertspoonfuls of the mixture into the pan, spacing them slightly apart, and fry for 3–4 minutes, turning once, until golden. Transfer to a serving plate and keep warm while frying the remainder of the potato mixture. (If broiling the potato scones, put them on an oiled, foil-lined baking sheet and cook under a preheated broiler for 5 minutes, turning once halfway through the cooking time.) Serve warm.

Energy: 68 kcals/287 kJ **Protein:** 2 g
Carbohydrate: 8 g **Fat:** 3 g **Fiber:** 1 g
Calcium: 15 mg **Iron:** <1 mg

Millet, fruit, and nut granola

Serves 4 • **Preparation:** 3 minutes • **Cooking:** 2 minutes

½ cup millet flakes

3 tablespoons chopped nuts

¼ cup golden raisins

¼ cup dried apricots, prunes, or dates, chopped

⅓ cup unsweetened shredded coconut

¼ cup sunflower seeds

3 tablespoons flax seeds

1 Put the millet and nuts in a heavy skillet and cook over a gentle heat, stirring frequently, for 2–3 minutes until they begin to brown. Tip them into a bowl and allow to cool for 10 minutes.

2 Add the dried fruits, coconut, and seeds and mix together well. Store in a jar or bowl for up to one week. Serve with either milk or fruit juice.

VARIATION

The quantities of fruit and nuts in this nutritious cereal can be varied or substituted with other ingredients to suit personal taste and preferences.

Energy: 289 kcals/1208 kJ   Protein: 7 g
Carbohydrate: 35 g   Fat: 14 g   Fiber: 7 g
Calcium: 42 mg   Iron: 2 mg

Spiced apple porridge

Serves 1 • **Preparation:** 1 minute • **Cooking:** 3–4 minutes

1 cup apple juice

½ teaspoon ground cinnamon

2 tablespoons millet flakes

TO SERVE

thick yogurt

Demerara sugar (optional)

VARIATION

For a change, try using fresh orange juice instead of apple juice, adding a little honey for extra sweetness if necessary.

1 Put the apple juice and cinnamon in a heatproof serving bowl. Sprinkle in the millet flakes and stir gently.

2 Microwave on full power for 3–4 minutes, stirring frequently until thick and creamy. Serve with spoonfuls of yogurt and, if you like your porridge sweet, sprinkled with sugar.

TIP

To cook the porridge in a saucepan, put the ingredients into a small pan and heat gently, stirring frequently, for 6–8 minutes until thick and creamy. Add a little extra juice if the mixture becomes dry.

Energy: 174 kcals/739 kJ   Protein: 2 g
Carbohydrate: 40 g   Fat: 1 g   Fiber: 2 g
Calcium: 50 mg   Iron: 1 mg

Breakfast cereal bars

Makes 16 • **Preparation:** 10 minutes • **Cooking:** 25–30 minutes

½ cup butter, softened

2 tablespoons light brown sugar

2 tablespoons light corn syrup

½ cup millet flakes

¼ cup quinoa

⅓ cup dried cherries or cranberries

½ cup golden raisins

¼ cup sunflower seeds

3 tablespoons sesame seeds

3 tablespoons flax seeds

½ cup unsweetened shredded coconut

2 eggs, lightly beaten

1 Grease an 11 x 8 inch shallow rectangular baking pan. Beat together the butter, sugar, and syrup until creamy.

2 Add all the remaining ingredients and beat well until combined. Turn into the pan and level the surface with the back of a dessertspoon.

3 Bake in a preheated oven, 350°F, for 35 minutes until deep golden. Allow to cool in the pan.

4 Turn out onto a wooden board and carefully cut into 16 bars using a serrated knife. Store in an airtight container for up to 5 days.

TIP

These crumbly breakfast bars are a much healthier alternative to store-bought cereal bars. Not only are they ideal for quick breakfasts, they make great snacks or lunch box fillers, too.

Energy: 156 kcals/650 kJ **Protein:** 3 g
Carbohydrate: 16 g **Fat:** 9 g **Fiber:** 1 g
Calcium: 54 mg **Iron:** 1 mg

Homemade bread

Makes 1 small loaf • **Preparation:** 5 minutes • **Cooking:** see manual

1½ cups water

1 teaspoon salt

1 tablespoon butter, melted

1 tablespoon superfine sugar

4 cups gluten-free bread mix
   for bread machines

2 tablespoons sesame seeds

2 tablespoons sunflower seeds

1 tablespoon poppy seeds

1 teaspoon instant dried yeast

1 Put all the ingredients into the bread machine bucket, following the order and method given in the manual, and adding the seeds with the flour.

2 Fit the bucket into the machine and set to the program and crust setting recommended for breads.

3 Once baked, transfer to a wire rack to cool.

Making bread by hand

Preparation: 5 minutes, plus rising • **Cooking:** 20–25 minutes

Mix 1½ teaspoons instant dried yeast with 1 tablespoon superfine sugar and 1 cup tepid water and milk, mixed. Leave for 5 minutes until frothy. Sift 1 cup brown or white rice flour, ½ cup potato flour, and ½ cup cornmeal into a bowl. Add ½ teaspoon salt, 1 beaten egg, 2 tablespoons olive oil, and the yeast mixture, then stir to make a smooth, stiff batter. Turn into a greased 2 lb nonstick loaf pan. Secure inside a large plastic bag and leave in a warm place to rise for about 45 minutes or until risen to the top of the pan. Bake in a preheated oven, 400°F, for 20–25 minutes until firm. Transfer to a wire rack to cool.

Energy: 213 kcals/895 kJ   **Protein:** 2 g
Carbohydrate: 43 g   **Fat:** 4 g   **Fiber:** 3 g
Calcium: 21 mg   **Iron:** <1 mg

Breakfast cornbread

Makes 8 slices • **Preparation:** 5 minutes • **Cooking:** 25–30 minutes

1 cup fine cornmeal

½ cup chickpea flour

1½ teaspoons Gluten-free
baking powder
(see page 42)

1 egg

2 tablespoons butter,
melted

1 cup whole or lowfat milk

salt and pepper

VARIATION

For a larger loaf, double up
on the ingredients and bake
in a 2 lb loaf pan. Add an
extra 10 minutes to the
cooking time.

1 Lightly oil a 1 lb loaf pan. Put the cornmeal, flour,
baking powder, and a little salt and pepper in a bowl
and make a well in the center. Beat the egg with the
butter and milk and add a little to the bowl.

2 Beat with a whisk, gradually incorporating the dry
ingredients to make a smooth paste. Add the
remaining milk mixture and beat until smooth.

3 Turn into the prepared pan and bake in a preheated
oven, 325°F, for 25–30 minutes until just firm. Leave in
the pan for 10 minutes, before transfering to a wire
rack to cool.

TIP

This quick and easy bread is delicious simply
spread with butter or topped with scrambled or
poached eggs.

Energy: 130 kcals/545 kJ   **Protein:** 5 g
Carbohydrate: 15 g   **Fat:** 6 g   **Fiber:** 1 g
Calcium: 60 mg   **Iron:** <1 mg

Cranberry, banana, and sesame smoothie

Makes 1 large or 2 small glasses • **Preparation:** 2 minutes

⅓ cup dried cranberries

juice of ½ lemon

1 large banana

1 tablespoon sesame seeds

2 tablespoons thick yogurt

¾ cup whole or lowfat milk

1 Put the cranberries and lemon juice in a food processor or blender and process until the berries are in small pieces.

2 Add the banana and sesame seeds and process to a puree, scraping the mixture down from the sides of the bowl at intervals if necessary.

3 Add the yogurt and milk, processing until smooth and frothy, then pour into a glass.

Energy: 420 kcals/1765 kJ **Protein:** 16 g
Carbohydrate: 45 g **Fat:** 21 g **Fiber:** 10 g
Calcium: 478 mg **Iron:** 2.5 mg

Mango, orange, and soy milkshake

Makes 1 large or 2 small glasses • **Preparation:** 3 minutes

1 small ripe mango

juice of 1 orange

⅔ cup soy milk

1–2 teaspoons honey

1 Halve the mango and discard the pit. Scoop the flesh into a food processor or blender.

2 Add the orange juice, soy milk, and 1 teaspoon of the honey. Process until smooth, scraping the mixture down from the sides of the bowl if necessary.

3 Taste for sweetness and, if it is needed, add a little more honey, then pour the milkshake into a glass.

Energy: 200 kcals/853 kJ **Protein:** 6 g
Carbohydrate: 40 g **Fat:** 3 g **Fiber:** 5 g
Calcium: 50 mg **Iron:** 2 mg

Spicy fruit and seed bread

Makes 1 x 1 lb loaf • **Preparation:** 10 minutes • **Cooking:** 20–25 minutes

1 cup chickpea flour

1 cup gluten-free flour

2 teaspoons instant dried yeast

1 teaspoon salt

1 teaspoon superfine sugar

1 tablespoon black onion seeds

1 tablespoon cumin seeds

2 teaspoons ground coriander

¼ teaspoon crushed red pepper

⅓ cup dried mango or pear, chopped

2 tablespoons refined peanut oil

¾ cup hand-hot water

1 Put the flours, yeast, salt, sugar, spices, and dried fruit in a bowl and mix together.

2 Add the oil and water and mix to a stiff paste.

3 Turn into a greased 1 lb loaf pan, cover loosely with oiled plastic wrap, and leave in a warm place for about 45 minutes until the mixture rises slightly above the top of the pan. Remove the plastic wrap.

4 Bake in a preheated oven, 400°F, for 20–25 minutes until firm to the touch. Loosen the edges of the loaf with a knife and turn out onto a wire rack to cool.

TIP

With its lovely crumbly texture and intense flavors, this tasty bread makes a perfect lunch served with a simple tomato, onion, and soft cheese salad.

 Energy: 172 kcals/727 kJ   Protein: 6 g
Carbohydrate: 30 g   Fat: 5 g   Fiber: 4 g
Calcium: 55 mg   Iron: 3 mg

Toasted open sandwiches

Serves 2 • **Preparation:** 5 minutes • **Cooking:** 2 minutes

2 garlic cloves, crushed

3 tablespoons olive oil

4 slices gluten-free bread

1½ cups roasted peppers

3½ oz firm goat cheese,
   thinly sliced

black olives

1 tablespoon balsamic vinegar

salt and pepper

VARIATION

You can vary the toppings to suit your taste. Try a layer of ready-made pesto topped with halved cherry tomatoes and canned navy beans, drained and rinsed. Drizzle with olive oil and balsamic vinegar.

1 Mix the garlic with 2 tablespoons of the olive oil and a little seasoning. Put the bread on a baking sheet and toast it on one side. Turn the slices over, brush with the garlic oil and toast until golden.

2 Arrange the roasted peppers over the bread and top with the goat cheese slices. Return to the broiler and cook for about 1 minute to heat through.

3 Transfer the sandwiches to serving plates. Sprinkle the portions with several black olives and drizzle with the remaining olive oil and balsamic vinegar.

Energy: 570 kcals/2117 kJ **Protein:** 9 g
Carbohydrate: 35 g **Fat:** 37 g **Fiber:** 4 g
Calcium: 149 mg **Iron:** 1 mg

Chickpea flatbreads

Serves 4 • Preparation: 20 minutes • **Cooking:** about 20 minutes

FLATBREADS

1 cup chickpea flour

½ cup gluten-free flour

¼ teaspoon salt

2 tablespoons olive oil

5–6 tablespoons milk

FILLING

1 large eggplant, thinly sliced

2 zucchini, thinly sliced

2 tablespoons olive oil

2 tablespoons finely chopped
   oregano or rosemary

6 tablespoons sun-dried
   tomato paste

4 large tomatoes, thinly sliced

salt and pepper

1 To make the flatbreads, put the flours, salt, and oil in a bowl. Add 5 tablespoons of the milk and mix with a round-bladed knife to a firm dough, adding a little more milk if the mixture is too dry. Knead lightly until smooth, then set aside.

2 Arrange the eggplant and zucchini slices on a large foil-lined baking sheet. Season lightly and brush with a little oil. Sprinkle the herbs on top and broil for 6–8 minutes until golden. Turn the slices over, brush with the remaining oil, and broil the other side until golden.

3 Divide the chickpea dough into 4 pieces. Roll 1 piece out very thinly on a well-floured surface to a 9 inch round, turning the dough frequently so it does not stick to the surface. Shape the remaining pieces in the same way.

4 Brush a large skillet with a little oil and fry the flatbreads individually for about 1 minute on each side.

5 Spread with the tomato paste and arrange the eggplant, zucchini, and tomato slices on top. Season and roll up to serve.

Energy: 430 kcals/1796 kJ **Protein:** 12 g
Carbohydrate: 42 g **Fat:** 25 g **Fiber:** 10 g
Calcium: 124 mg **Iron:** 5 mg

Baked sweet potatoes with tomato salsa

Serves 2 • Preparation: 5 minutes **• Cooking:** 45 minutes

2 large sweet potatoes, each about 9 oz

1 tablespoon olive oil

2 large tomatoes

½ small red onion, finely chopped

1 celery stick, finely chopped

small handful fresh cilantro, chopped

2 tablespoons lime juice

2 teaspoons superfine sugar

½ cup grated Emmental or cheddar cheese

salt

1 Scrub the potatoes and put them in a small roasting pan. Prick with a fork and drizzle with the oil and a little salt. Bake in a preheated oven, 400°F, for 45 minutes until tender.

2 Meanwhile, finely chop the tomatoes and mix in a bowl with the onion, celery, cilantro, lime juice, and sugar.

3 Halve the potatoes and fluff up the flesh with a fork. Sprinkle with the cheese and serve topped with the salsa.

TIP
If you do not have the time to bake the potatoes, they can be microwaved like ordinary ones, although this way you will lose the wonderful crispy baked flavor. Prick them with a fork and cook on the highest setting for 15–20 minutes, or according to the manufacturer's instructions.

Energy: 434 kcals/1835 kJ **Protein:** 12 g
Carbohydrate: 69 g **Fat:** 14 g **Fiber:** 9 g
Calcium: 333 mg **Iron:** 3 mg

Potato rosti

Serves 4 • **Preparation:** 10 minutes • **Cooking:** 10 minutes

2 lb small baking potatoes, unpeeled

1 small onion, thinly sliced

1 tablespoon butter

2 tablespoons olive oil

salt and pepper

1 Leave the potatoes whole and cook in boiling, salted water for 10 minutes until softened but not completely tender. Drain and allow to cool.

2 Peel the skins from the potatoes and coarsely grate the flesh into a bowl. Stir in the onion and a little seasoning.

3 Heat the butter with the oil in a medium, heavy, preferably nonstick skillet. Tip the potato mixture into the pan and spread it in an even layer. Cook gently for about 10 minutes or until it is turning golden around the edges.

4 Shake the pan to loosen the potatoes, then, with a plate over the top, invert the pan so the potato cake comes out. Slide it back into the pan to cook the other side and fry for an additional 10 minutes until it is done on the underside. Serve in wedges.

TIP

These crisp and golden rostis make an excellent base for tangy dressed bean or fish salads, or simply ham and eggs.

Energy: 270 kcals/1134 kJ   Protein: 5 g
Carbohydrate: 44 g   Fat: 9 g   Fiber: 9 g
Calcium: 17 mg   Iron: 1 mg

Mascarpone, feta, and herb pâté

Serves 6 • Preparation: 10 minutes

1 cup mascarpone cheese

6–8 tablespoons milk

7 oz feta cheese, cut into
small dice

½ celery stick, finely diced

⅓ cup pitted black olives,
roughly chopped

2 scallions, finely chopped

2 garlic cloves, crushed

1 tablespoon fresh
chopped mint

1 tablespoon fresh chopped
flat leaf parsley

salt and pepper

1 Put the mascarpone into a bowl and beat lightly to
soften. Stir in sufficient milk to give the consistency
of thick yogurt.

2 Add the feta cheese to the bowl with the celery,
olives, scallions, garlic, herbs, and seasoning,
and gently fold the ingredients together until
evenly combined.

3 Turn into a serving bowl, cover, and chill until ready
to serve.

Energy: 270 kcals/1119 kJ **Protein:** 9 g
Carbohydrate: 3 g **Fat:** 25 g **Fiber:** 0 g
Calcium: 156 mg **Iron:** <1 mg

Chili rice noodles

Serves 2 • **Preparation:** 5 minutes • **Cooking:** 3 minutes

4 teaspoons seasoned
rice vinegar

1 tablespoon superfine sugar

1 teaspoon Thai fish sauce

1 tablespoon soy sauce

3½ oz dried rice ribbon
noodles

1 tablespoon vegetable oil or
refined peanut oil

1 small red chili, seeded and
finely shredded

1 small red bell pepper, seeded
and finely shredded

½ cup snow peas, sliced thinly
lengthwise

1 Mix together the vinegar, sugar, fish sauce, and soy sauce. Put the noodles in a bowl and cover them with boiling water. Leave for 3–4 minutes until soft.

2 While the noodles are soaking, heat the oil in a skillet and fry the chili, red pepper, and snow peas for 3 minutes until softened.

3 Drain the noodles and add to the pan with the sauce mixture. Toss together and serve immediately.

TIP

Keep an eye on the noodles during soaking as they quickly become too soft. You must use them as soon as they are drained—they will stick together if left in the colander.

VARIATION

Try scallions, sugarsnap peas, mushrooms, or green beans instead of peppers and snow peas.

Energy: 283 kcals/1180 kJ   **Protein:** 4 g
Carbohydrate: 52 g   **Fat:** 6 g   **Fiber:** 2 g
Calcium: 29 mg   **Iron:** 2 mg

Spiced and salted nuts

Makes 3 cups • **Preparation:** 3 minutes • **Cooking:** 3–4 minutes

1 tablespoon butter

1 tablespoon light olive oil

3 cups whole mixed nuts
(e.g. almonds, hazelnuts,
walnuts, brazil nuts)

1 tablespoon ground paprika

½ teaspoon cayenne pepper

2 teaspoons cumin seeds,
lightly crushed

sea salt flakes, for sprinkling

1 Melt the butter with the oil in a skillet. Add the nuts
and spices.

2 Gently fry the mixture, stirring continuously until the
nuts are lightly browned.

3 Remove from the heat and cool slightly. Strain with a
slotted spoon into a bowl and season with salt. Store
in an airtight container for up to one week.

TIP
For a milder flavor, reduce the quantity of cayenne
pepper to ½ teaspoon.

Energy: 286 kcals/1180 kJ   **Protein:** 7 g
Carbohydrate: 2 g   **Fat:** 28 g   **Fiber:** 4 g
Calcium: 67 mg   **Iron:** 1.5 mg

Hummus

Serves 6 • **Preparation:** 15 minutes, plus overnight soaking • **Cooking:** about 1 hour

1 cup dried chickpeas

juice of 2 lemons

3 garlic cloves, roughly chopped

3 tablespoons olive oil

²/₃ cup tahini paste

salt and pepper

extra olive oil, to drizzle (optional)

1 Put the chickpeas in a bowl, cover with plenty of water, and allow to soak overnight. Drain and put in a saucepan with plenty of fresh water. Bring to a boil and boil rapidly for 10 minutes. Reduce the heat and simmer gently for 45–60 minutes until the chickpeas are completely tender. Drain well.

2 Tip the chickpeas into a food processor and process to a paste. Add the lemon juice, garlic, olive oil, tahini paste, and seasoning, and blend until very smooth, scraping the mixture down from the sides of the bowl when necessary. The longer it is blended, the creamier the hummus will become.

3 Transfer to a serving bowl, cover, and chill until ready to serve. Serve drizzled with extra olive oil if desired.

TIP

Homemade hummus is a delicious and versatile treat to have in the refrigerator. It can be used as a sandwich filler, as a topping for baked potatoes, or as a simple snack with vegetable sticks.

Energy: 284 kcals/1180 kJ   **Protein:** 10 g
Carbohydrate: 13 g   **Fat:** 22 g   **Fiber:** 3 g
Calcium: 212 mg   **Iron:** 4 mg

Potato and onion tortilla

Serves 6 • Preparation: 10 minutes • **Cooking:** 30 minutes

1½ lb baking potatoes

4 tablespoons olive oil

2 large onions, thinly sliced

6 eggs, beaten

salt and pepper

VARIATION

Thinly sliced chorizo sausage, grated Parmesan cheese, garlic, fresh herbs, and chopped sweet peppers all make delicious additions to a tortilla. Mix them in with the onions.

1 Slice the potatoes very thinly and toss them in a bowl with a little seasoning. Heat the oil in a medium, heavy skillet. Add the potatoes and fry them very gently for 10 minutes, turning them frequently until they are softened but not browned.

2 Add the onions and fry them gently for an additional 5 minutes without browning. Spread the potatoes and onions in an even layer in the pan and turn the heat down as low as possible.

3 Pour over the eggs, cover, and cook very gently for about 15 minutes until the eggs have set. (If the center of the omelet is too wet, put the pan under a moderate broiler to finish cooking.) Tip the tortilla on to a plate and serve warm or cold.

TIP

Serve for a family lunch or supper with salad, chilling any leftovers for lunch boxes or snacks the following day.

Energy: 296 kcals/1237 kJ   **Protein:** 13 g
Carbohydrate: 28 g   **Fat:** 16 g   **Fiber:** 3 g
Calcium: 68 mg   **Iron:** 2 mg

Potato pizza margherita

Serves 3–4 • Preparation: 20 minutes • Cooking: 45 minutes

2 lb baking potatoes

3 tablespoons olive oil

1 egg, beaten

½ cup freshly grated Parmesan or cheddar cheese

4 tablespoons sun-dried tomato paste or ketchup

1 lb small tomatoes, thinly sliced

4 oz mozzarella cheese, thinly sliced

1 tablespoon fresh chopped thyme (optional)

salt

1 Cut the potatoes into small chunks and cook in boiling, lightly salted water for about 15 minutes until tender. Drain thoroughly, return to the pan, and allow to cool for 10 minutes. Oil a large baking sheet.

2 Add 2 tablespoons of the oil, the egg, and half the grated cheese to the potato, and mix well. Turn out onto the prepared baking sheet and spread to a 10 inch round. Bake in a preheated oven, 400°F, for 15 minutes.

3 Remove from the oven and spread with the tomato paste or ketchup. Arrange the tomato and mozzarella slices on top. Sprinkle with the remaining grated cheese, thyme if using, and a little salt. Drizzle with the remaining oil.

4 Return to the oven for 15 minutes more until the potato is crisp around the edges and the cheese is melting.

TIP
Mini potato pizzas are a great idea for children's parties. Simply divide the potato mixture into six circles on a baking sheet.

Energy: 633 kcals/2655 kJ   Protein: 28 g
Carbohydrate: 70 g   Fat: 28 g   Fiber: 8 g
Calcium: 93 mg   Iron: 1 mg

Homemade veggie sausages and beans

Serves 6 • Preparation: 30 minutes, plus overnight soaking • **Cooking:** about 2 hours

1¼ cups dried navy beans

2 teaspoons cornstarch

1¼ cups vegetable stock

2 tablespoons olive oil

2 onions, chopped

13 oz can chopped tomatoes

1 tablespoon grainy mustard

2 tablespoons molasses

2 tablespoons tomato
  ketchup

SAUSAGES

10 oz potatoes

2 small carrots, finely grated

1 large onion, finely chopped

1 cup grated cheddar cheese

2 cups gluten-free bread
  crumbs

1 egg

salt and pepper

a little oil for frying

1 Soak the beans overnight in plenty of cold water. Drain, put in a pan, and cover with fresh water. Boil rapidly for 10 minutes, then reduce the heat and simmer gently for 30 minutes until tender. Drain and turn into a casserole dish.

2 Blend the cornstarch with 4 tablespoons of water until smooth. Add the stock and pour over the beans. Then add the oil, onions, tomatoes, mustard, molasses, and ketchup, stirring everything together to mix well. Cook in a preheated oven, 325°F, for 1½–2 hours until the beans are tender and the sauce thickened.

3 Meanwhile, make the sausages. Dice the potato and cook in boiling water for 5 minutes until soft. Drain thoroughly, return to the pan, and mash until smooth.

4 Turn the mash into a bowl and add the remaining ingredients (apart from the oil). Season lightly and mix together thoroughly. Divide into 12 portions and shape each into a thick sausage.

5 Heat the oil in a skillet and cook the sausages for about 10 minutes turning frequently until golden. Serve with the beans.

Energy: 409 kcals/1722 kJ   Protein: 18 g
Carbohydrate: 55 g   Fat: 14 g   Fiber: 7 g
Calcium: 290 mg   Iron: 5 mg

Little cottage pies

Serves 8–10 • **Preparation:** 25 minutes • **Cooking:** 1 hour 10 minutes

2 onions, very roughly
chopped

13 oz carrots, cut into large
pieces

4 celery sticks, cut into chunks

¼ cup butter

2 tablespoons olive oil

1 lb 2 oz lean ground lamb

2 cups chicken or lamb stock

4 tablespoons tomato ketchup

2 tablespoons chopped
oregano or rosemary

4 lb large potatoes

⅔ cup whole milk

13 oz can baked beans

salt and pepper

1 Put the onions, carrots, and celery in a food
processor and process until very finely chopped. Heat
half the butter with the oil in a large saucepan, add
the vegetables, and fry, stirring for 5 minutes until they
begin to brown. Add the meat and fry, breaking it up
with a wooden spoon for an additional 5 minutes.

2 Add the stock, ketchup, herb, and a little seasoning,
and bring to a boil. Reduce the heat, cover with a lid,
and simmer gently for 20 minutes, stirring occasionally.

3 Meanwhile, cut the potatoes into chunks and cook in
lightly salted, boiling water for 15–20 minutes until
tender. Drain and return to the saucepan. Mash well
and stir in the remaining butter and the milk.

4 Stir the baked beans into the meat mixture. Turn into
a large, shallow ovenproof dish or individual foil or pie
dishes. Spoon the potatoes over the filling, spreading
it right to the edges.

5 Bake in a preheated oven, 400°F, for about 40 minutes
until the potato is pale golden.

Energy: 470 kcals/1970 kJ   Protein: 24 g
Carbohydrate: 62 g   Fat: 16 g   Fiber: 10 g
Calcium: 100 mg   Iron: 3 mg

Corn and bacon muffins

Makes 12 • Preparation: 10 minutes • **Cooking:** 20 minutes

6 bacon slices

1 small red onion, finely chopped

1¼ cups frozen corn kernals

1 cup fine cornmeal

1 cup gluten-free all-purpose flour

2 teaspoons Gluten-free baking powder (see page 42)

½ cup grated cheddar cheese

¾ cup lowfat milk

2 eggs

3 tablespoons vegetable oil

1 Lightly oil a 12-cup muffin pan. Cut off any rind and excess fat, then finely chop the bacon and dry-fry it in a pan with the onion over a moderate heat for 3–4 minutes until the bacon is turning crisp. Cook the corn in boiling water for 2 minutes to soften.

2 Put the cornmeal, flour, and baking powder in a bowl and mix together. Add the corn, cheese, bacon, and onions, and stir in.

3 Beat the milk with the eggs and oil and add to the bowl. Stir gently until combined, then divide among the pan cups.

4 Bake in a preheated oven, 425°F, for 15–20 minutes until golden and just firm. Loosen the edges of the muffins with a knife and transfer to a wire rack to cool.

VARIATION

For a vegetarian version, replace the bacon with an extra ¼ cup cheese and add salt and pepper.

Energy: 228 kcals/954 kJ   Protein: 7 g
Carbohydrate: 26 g   Fat: 11 g   Fiber: 1 g
Calcium: 68 mg   Iron: 1 mg

Sticky chicken drumsticks

Makes 16 drumsticks • **Preparation:** 5 minutes • **Cooking:** 50 minutes

16 chicken drumsticks

4 tablespoons honey

finely grated zest and juice
of 1 lemon

finely grated zest and juice
of 1 orange

3 tablespoons Worcestershire
sauce

4 tablespoons tomato ketchup

1 Make several diagonal cuts through the fleshy part of each chicken drumstick and arrange in a single layer in a roasting pan or shallow ovenproof dish.

2 Mix together the remaining ingredients and spoon over the chicken. Cover and chill until ready to cook.

3 Cook in a preheated oven, 350°F, for about 50 minutes, turning the chicken and basting frequently until the chicken is cooked through and thickly coated with the sticky glaze. Serve hot or chill thoroughly for serving cold.

TIP

For the perfect accompaniment make some homemade oven fries. Scrub 2 lb baking potatoes, cut them into small wedges, and put them in one layer in a roasting pan. Drizzle with vegetable oil and season with salt, turning the potatoes so they are well covered in oil. Bake with the chicken until they are pale golden.

Energy: 133 kcals/558 kJ   Protein: 15 g
Carbohydrate: 7 g   Fat: 5 g   Fiber: 0 g
Calcium: 16 mg   Iron: 1 mg

Chocolate fudge crisps

Makes 24 • **Preparation:** 15 minutes • **Cooking:** 2 minutes

3 oz fudge

3 oz milk chocolate

⅓ cup unsalted butter

3 tablespoons light corn syrup

¼ cup cocoa powder

5 cups puffed rice cereal

VARIATION

Substitute ⅔ cup raisins for the fudge if preferred.

1 Place 24 paper bake cups on a large tray or baking sheet. Chop the fudge and chocolate into small dice and set aside.

2 Put the butter and syrup in a large saucepan and heat gently, stirring until the butter melts. Stir in the cocoa powder and remove from the heat. Stir in the cereal until well coated.

3 Add the chopped chocolate and fudge to the mixture. Spoon into the cases, packing the mixture down gently, and allow to set. Store in an airtight container for up to 3 days.

Energy: 89 kcals/373 kJ **Protein:** 1 g
Carbohydrate: 13 g **Fat:** 4 g **Fiber:** 0 g
Calcium: 14 mg **Iron:** <1 mg

Flower cupcakes

Makes 18 • **Preparation:** 25 minutes, plus cooling • **Cooking:** 25 minutes

½ cup ground almonds

¾ cup gluten-free all-purpose flour

1 teaspoon Gluten-free baking powder (see page 42)

½ cup unsalted butter, softened

½ cup superfine sugar

2 eggs

finely grated zest of 1 lemon, plus 3 tablespoons juice

2 cups confectioners' sugar

orange and yellow food coloring

VARIATION

If you'd prefer to leave out the nuts, use an additional ½ cup gluten-free flour instead.

1 Line tartlet pans with 18 paper bake cups.

2 Put the almonds, flour, baking powder, butter, sugar, eggs, and lemon zest in a large bowl. Beat with a hand-held electric mixer for about 2 minutes until smooth and creamy.

3 Using teaspoons, divide the mixture among the paper cups. Bake in a preheated oven at 350°F, for 20–25 minutes until golden and just firm to touch. Transfer to a wire rack to cool.

4 To decorate, put the lemon juice in a bowl and beat in the confectioners' sugar to make a smooth paste. Transfer half to another bowl and color one half orange, the other yellow.

5 Put a dessertspoonful of each color icing in a plastic bag and squeeze into a corner. Cut off the merest tip to make a pastry bag. Spoon the remaining icing over the cakes,spreading to the corners with a spatula.

6 Using the icing in the bags, pipe simple flower shapes over the cakes so the colors contrast. Alternatively pipe the children's initials or a message onto the cakes.

Energy: 169 kcals/710 kJ   **Protein:** 2 g
Carbohydrate: 24 g   **Fat:** 8 g   **Fiber:** 1 g
Calcium: 18 mg   **Iron:** 0 mg

Rainbow popsicles

Makes 12 • Preparation: 20 minutes

1 large ripe mango

4 kiwi fruit

2 cups strawberries

3 cups blackberries or
  blueberries

VARIATION

Almost any fruit can be used for popsicles, as long as it is really ripe and therefore soft and sweet. If you do not have the time to make layered popsicles, simply use a selection of different flavors. Stir in a little honey or sugar to sweeten the fruits, if desired.

1 Halve the mango and discard the pit. Scoop the flesh into a food processor or blender and process to a smooth puree, scraping the fruit down from the sides of the bowl if necessary.

2 Pour into a small pitcher (if the mixture is too thick to pour, thin with a little orange juice or water). Quarter-fill 12 popsicle molds with the mango juice and put in the freezer for about 30 minutes or until set.

3 Meanwhile, prepare the other fruit. Peel the kiwi fruit, puree, and put in a clean pitcher. Hull and blend the strawberries, then press through a sieve over a bowl to remove the seeds. Blend the blackberries or blueberries and press through a sieve into a separate bowl.

4 Pour a layer of kiwi juice over the mango and return to the freezer. Add the strawberry puree, pushing in the popsicle sticks once it is beginning to freeze. Finish with the blackberry or blueberry layer and return to the freezer, where the popsicles can be kept for up to 6 months.

5 To serve, run the molds quickly under very hot water to loosen the popsicles, then gently pull them out.

Energy: 30 kcals/133 kJ   **Protein:** 1 g
Carbohydrate: 7 g   **Fat:** 0 g   **Fiber:** 3 g
Calcium: 23 mg   **Iron:** 0.5 mg

Chocolate cookie log

Makes about 20 slices • **Preparation:** 10 minutes • **Cooking:** 2 minutes

1 tablespoon peanut oil

¼ cup popping corn

3½ oz milk chocolate

3½ oz semisweet chocolate

2 tablespoons butter

½ cup nuts and raisins

⅓ cup white chocolate
   chips

VARIATION

For a more sophisticated
adult version, you could use
7 oz semisweet chocolate
instead of the mix of milk
and semisweet, and milk
chocolate rather than
white chocolate chips.

1 To make the popcorn, heat the oil in a heavy
saucepan with a tight-fitting lid. Add the corn and
heat very gently until the corn starts to pop, shaking
the pan frequently.

2 Once the popping subsides, remove the pan from the
heat and wait for a minute or so until the popping
stops completely. Measure out 5 cups of the corn.
Once it is cool enough to handle, crush it with your
hands into smaller pieces over a bowl.

3 Melt the chocolate with the butter in a large bowl. Stir
in the crushed corn and nuts and raisins until evenly
combined. Gently stir in the chocolate chips.

4 Lay a sheet of parchment paper on your surface and
spoon the chocolate mixture across the center. Bring
the paper up around the chocolate mixture, shaping
and packing it into a roll about 12 inches long. Chill
for at least 2 hours until firm.

5 To serve, unwrap the roll and cut into chunky slices
with a sharp knife.

Energy: 119 kcals/495 kJ   **Protein:** 2 g
Carbohydrate: 11 g   **Fat:** 8 g   **Fiber:** 0 g
Calcium: 22 mg   **Iron:** <1 mg

Chocolate lover's birthday cake

Serves 12–14 • **Preparation:** 30 minutes, plus cooling • **Cooking:** 25 minutes

¾ cup unsalted butter, softened

¾ cup superfine sugar

3 eggs

2 teaspoons vanilla extract

¼ cup cocoa powder

1½ cups gluten-free flour

1 teaspoon Gluten-free baking powder (see page 42)

3½ oz milk chocolate, chopped

FROSTING

7 oz semisweet chocolate

4 tablespoons milk

3 tablespoons unsalted butter

1½ cups confectioners' sugar

selection of small chocolates or candy bars, cut into chunks, to decorate

cocoa powder and confectioners' sugar, to dust

1 Grease and line the bases of a couple of 8 inch round layer pans.

2 Put the butter, sugar, eggs, vanilla, cocoa powder, flour, and baking powder in a mixing bowl and beat for about 2 minutes until smooth and creamy.

3 Divide between the prepared pans, sprinkle with the chopped milk chocolate and level the surfaces. Bake in a preheated oven, 350°F, for 25 minutes or until firm to the touch. Transfer to a wire rack to cool.

4 To finish the cake, break up the semisweet chocolate and put in a saucepan with the milk and butter. Heat over the lowest setting until melted, stirring frequently. Beat in the confectioners' sugar until smooth.

5 Use a little of the frosting to sandwich the cakes together and transfer to a serving plate. Spread the remaining frosting over the top and sides of the cakes, swirling with a spatula.

6 Position the candles, if using, and pile plenty of chocolate around the edges to decorate, pressing the pieces gently into the frosting. Lightly dust with cocoa power and confectioners' sugar.

Energy: 460 kcals/19290 kJ   **Protein:** 5 g
Carbohydrate: 59 g   **Fat:** 24 g   **Fiber:** <1 g
Calcium: 48 mg   **Iron:** 1 mg

Chicken and ham soup

Serves 8 • **Preparation:** 20 minutes • **Cooking:** 1 hour, 20 minutes

12 oz piece lean ham

3 tablespoons olive oil

4 large chicken thighs, skinned

3 medium onions, chopped

2 celery sticks, sliced

2 bay leaves

2½ cups chicken stock

12 oz potatoes, cut into small dice

1 cup frozen corn kernals

DUMPLINGS

¾ cup fine cornmeal

1 cup gluten-free flour

2 teaspoons Gluten-free baking powder (see page 42)

1 tablespoon chopped fresh thyme

⅜ stick chilled butter

salt and pepper

1 Chop the ham into ½ inch chunks. Heat the oil in a large, heavy saucepan. Add the chicken, onions, and celery, and fry gently for 10 minutes, stirring until golden.

2 Add the ham, bay leaves, stock, and 2½ cups water, and bring to a boil. Reduce the heat, cover, and simmer gently for 40 minutes until the chicken and ham are tender.

3 Pick out the chicken with a slotted spoon and, when cool enough to handle, shred the flesh from the bones. Return to the pan with the potatoes and corn. Simmer, covered, for 20 minutes, until the potatoes are tender.

4 To make the dumplings, mix together the cornmeal, flour, baking powder, thyme, and seasoning until evenly combined. Grate the butter into the mixture and add 1 cup water. Mix to a thick paste, adding a little more water if necessary.

5 Using 2 dessertspoons, roughly pat the paste into 8 rounds and spoon into the soup. Cover and simmer gently for about 10 minutes until the dumplings are light and puffy. Serve hot.

Energy: 334 kcals/1396 kJ **Protein:** 17 g
Carbohydrate: 36 g **Fat:** 14 g **Fiber:** 2 g
Calcium: 45 mg **Iron:** 2 mg

Parsnip and fresh ginger soup

Serves 6 • **Preparation:** 15 minutes • **Cooking:** 30 minutes

2 tablespoons butter

1½ lb parsnips, sliced

2 large onions, roughly chopped

5 cups chicken or vegetable stock

1 inch piece fresh ginger root, grated

¾ cup sour cream

salt and pepper (optional)

1 Melt the butter in a large saucepan. Add the parsnips and onions, and fry very gently for 10 minutes until softened but not browned.

2 Add the stock and bring to a boil. Reduce the heat, cover, and simmer gently for 20 minutes until the parsnips are tender. Stir in the ginger. Blend the mixture in a food processor or using a hand-held immersion blender until smooth.

3 Add half the sour cream and heat through, adding a little seasoning if desired. Ladle into soup bowls and swirl in the remaining sour cream to serve.

Energy: 268 kcals/1115 kJ   Protein: 4 g
Carbohydrate: 23 g   Fat: 18 g   Fiber: 7 g
Calcium: 73 mg   Iron: 1 mg

Lentil and rosemary soup

Serves 5–6 • **Preparation:** 10 minutes • **Cooking:** 45 minutes

1¼ cups green lentils

3 tablespoons olive oil

2 onions, chopped

3 garlic cloves, chopped

¼ teaspoon ground turmeric

1 tablespoon freshly chopped
  rosemary

2 bay leaves

3¾ cups vegetable stock

small handful chopped flat
  leaf parsley

salt and pepper

yogurt, to serve (optional)

1 Put the lentils in a saucepan, cover with water, and bring to a boil. Boil rapidly for 10 minutes, then drain.

2 Heat the oil in a large saucepan and fry the onions for 5 minutes until lightly browned. Add the garlic, turmeric, rosemary, bay leaves, lentils, and stock and bring to a boil.

3 Reduce the heat, cover, and simmer gently for about 30 minutes until the lentils are completely soft. Use a hand-held immersion blender to lightly pulp the soup, adding a little more stock if it becomes too thick. (Alternatively use a potato masher to pulp the mixture.)

4 Season to taste, stir in the parsley, and serve in bowls, with spoonfuls of yogurt, if desired.

Energy: 230 kcals/980 kJ   **Protein:** 13 g
Carbohydrate: 30 g   **Fat:** 8 g   **Fiber:** 1 g
Calcium: 57 mg   **Iron:** 6 mg

Chilled gazpacho

Serves 6 • **Preparation:** 20 minutes

1¾ lb tomatoes, skinned and
   roughly chopped

½ cucumber, roughly chopped

2 red bell peppers, seeded and
   roughly chopped

1 stick celery, chopped

2 garlic cloves, chopped

½ red chili, seeded and sliced

small handful fresh cilantro or
   flat leaf parsley

2 tablespoons white
   wine vinegar

2 tablespoons sun-dried
   tomato paste

4 tablespoons olive oil

ice cubes

salt

extra parsley or cilantro,
   to garnish

1 Mix together the vegetables, garlic, chili, and cilantro in a large bowl.

2 Add the vinegar, tomato paste, oil, and a little salt. Process in batches in a food processor or blender until smooth, scraping the mixture down from the sides of the bowl if necessary.

3 Collect the blended mixtures together in a clean bowl and check the seasoning, adding a little more salt if needed. Chill for up to 24 hours before serving.

4 To serve, ladle the gazpacho into large bowls, sprinkle with ice cubes and garnish with chopped parsley or cilantro.

TIP
Traditionally, gazpacho is served with little bowls of chopped garnishes such as hard-cooked egg, cucumber, pepper, parsley, and onion for sprinkling over the soup for extra flavor.

Energy: 135 kcals/560 kJ   Protein: 2 g
Carbohydrate: 8 g   Fat: 11 g   Fiber: 3 g
Calcium: 20 mg   Iron: 1 mg

Thai shrimp and noodle soup

Serves 4 • **Preparation:** 5 minutes • **Cooking:** 5 minutes

1 bunch scallions

7 oz bok choy or green cabbage

5 cups rich chicken stock

1 tablespoon light brown sugar

2 tablespoons seasoned rice vinegar

1 tablespoon soy sauce

2 tablespoons sesame oil

2 oz dried stir-fry rice noodles

2 inch piece fresh ginger root, finely chopped

7 oz peeled shrimp

1 Slice the scallions diagonally, then shred the bok choy or cabbage.

2 Put the stock, sugar, vinegar, and soy sauce in a large saucepan and bring to a boil.

3 Gently heat the oil in a skillet. Add the scallions and greens and cook very gently for 3 minutes to soften.

4 Break the noodles into short lengths and add to the stock with the vegetables, ginger, and shrimp. Heat through gently for 2 minutes and serve immediately.

Energy: 189 kcals/794 kJ **Protein:** 14 g
Carbohydrate: 18 g **Fat:** 7 g **Fiber:** 2 g
Calcium: 119 mg **Iron:** 2 mg

Millet "tabbouleh"

Serves 4–6 • **Preparation:** 10 minutes • **Cooking:** 10 minutes

1¼ cups millet

1 cup finely chopped flat
  leaf parsley

1 cup finely chopped mint

½ bunch scallions, finely sliced

⅓ cup pine nuts, toasted

½ cup red grapes, halved

2 tablespoons lemon juice

4 tablespoons extra virgin
  olive oil

salt and pepper

1 Cook the millet in plenty of boiling, lightly salted water for 10 minutes or until the grains are soft but not turning to a pulp. Strain through a sieve then pass under cold running water to cool. Drain thoroughly and tip into a salad bowl.

2 Stir in the remaining ingredients until well combined. Cover and chill to let the flavors mingle until ready to serve.

TIP

Here, millet replaces the bulgar wheat used traditionally in tabbouleh. It can be served with cold meats or cheese or used as a base for salad—try adding toasted seeds, chopped dried apricots or prunes, halved cherry tomatoes, sliced radishes, or lightly cooked vegetables such as asparagus and sugarsnap peas.

Energy: 429 kcals/1785 kJ   **Protein:** 6 g
Carbohydrate: 53 g   **Fat:** 21 g   **Fiber:** 1 g
Calcium: 53 mg   **Iron:** 2 mg

Walnut, pear, and green leaf salad

Serves 4 • **Preparation:** 10 minutes • **Cooking:** 3 minutes

¾ cup freshly grated Parmesan cheese

6 tablespoons walnut oil

2 tablespoons lemon juice

1 tablespoon grainy mustard

2 teaspoons superfine sugar

several fresh tarragon sprigs, roughly chopped

2 large, ripe pears

⅓ cup walnut pieces, lightly toasted

2½ cups mixed leaf salad (e.g. watercress, arugula, spinach)

salt and pepper

1 Oil a foil-lined baking sheet and sprinkle the Parmesan cheese over it, spreading it to a thin layer about 10 inches square. Cook under a preheated broiler for 2–3 minutes until the cheese has melted and is pale golden. Leave until cool enough to handle, then peel the foil away, letting the cheese break into pieces to form "croûtes."

2 Beat together the oil, lemon juice, mustard, sugar, tarragon, and seasoning. Halve and core the pears and cut into thin slices.

3 Toss the walnuts and pears with the salad leaves and dressing. Pile onto serving plates and sprinkle with the Parmesan croûtes.

VARIATION

Tarragon is lovely with sweet pears but other herbs, such as flat leaf parsley or fennel, also go well.

Energy: 395 kcals/1640 kJ   **Protein:** 11 g
Carbohydrate: 16 g   **Fat:** 32 g   **Fiber:** 2 g
Calcium: 300 mg   **Iron:** 2 mg

Buckwheat blinis with smoked fish

Serves 6 • Preparation: 20 minutes • Cooking: 10 minutes

BLINIS

1½ cups buckwheat flour

1 teaspoon Gluten-free baking powder (see page 42)

¼ teaspoon salt

2 eggs

1 cup whole milk

oil for frying

TO SERVE

2 tablespoons chopped fennel or tarragon

¾ cup sour cream

7 oz smoked salmon or trout

salt and pepper

TO GARNISH

lemon or lime wedges

fennel sprigs or chives

1 Mix together the buckwheat flour, baking powder, and salt in a bowl and make a well in the center.

2 Break the eggs into the well and add a little of the milk. Beat the milk and eggs together, gradually incorporating the flour to make a smooth paste. Beat in the remaining milk and pour into a pitcher.

3 Stir the herbs into the sour cream and season lightly to taste.

4 Heat a little oil in a large skillet over a low heat. Carefully pour some of the batter mixture into the pan so that it spreads to a small cake about 2½ inches in diameter. Pour several more pancakes into the pan, keeping them spaced slightly apart. Cook for 30–45 seconds until golden on the underside, then turn over with a spatula and cook for 1 minute more. Drain on paper towels and keep warm while cooking the remainder.

5 Place the blinis, 3 per serving, on plates and top each with a little sour cream. Lay pieces of smoked fish over the sour cream. Garnish with lemon or lime wedges and sprigs of herbs.

Energy: 363 kcals/1510 kJ   Protein: 15 g
Carbohydrate: 28 g   Fat: 22 g   Fiber: 2 g
Calcium: 77 mg   Iron: 1 mg

Fish cakes with fennel mayonnaise

Serves 4 • Preparation: 20 minutes • **Cooking:** 20 minutes

1 lb cod or haddock fillets, skin and bones removed

4 tablespoons milk

1½ lb baking potatoes

2 tablespoons butter

2 tablespoons capers, rinsed and chopped

1 medium egg

½ cup cornmeal

sunflower or light olive oil for frying

6 tablespoons mayonnaise

3 tablespoons plain yogurt

3 tablespoons freshly chopped fennel

2 teaspoons hot horseradish sauce

salt and pepper

1 Cut the fish into chunky pieces and put in a skillet with the milk and a little seasoning. Cover and cook gently for 5 minutes until just cooked through.

2 Meanwhile, cook the potatoes in boiling salted water for 15 minutes or until tender. Drain, tip into a bowl, and mash with a fork into chunky pieces.

3 Add the butter, capers, fish, 2 tablespoons of the cooking juices, and seasoning. Mix together until the ingredients are combined but the fish and potatoes are still chunky. Shape the mixture into 8–10 balls and flatten into cakes.

4 Lightly beat the egg on a plate. Sprinkle the cornmeal onto another plate. Coat the fish cakes first in the egg and then in the cornmeal.

5 Heat ½ inch of oil in a large skillet and fry the fish cakes, in batches if necessary, for about 2 minutes on each side until golden.

6 While they are cooking, mix together the mayonnaise, yogurt, fennel, and horseradish, and transfer to a serving dish. Serve with the hot fish cakes.

Energy: 667 kcals/2780 kJ   **Protein:** 32 g
Carbohydrate: 50 g   **Fat:** 39 g   **Fiber:** 3 g
Calcium: 123 mg   Iron: 2 mg

Baked trout with pine nuts

Serves 4 • Preparation: 10 minutes • Cooking: 15–20 minutes

butter for greasing

4 trout fillets, each about 4 oz, skinned

2 tablespoons olive oil

⅓ cup pine nuts

1 small onion, chopped

1 garlic clove, sliced

4 cups baby spinach

¼ cup freshly grated Parmesan cheese

salt and pepper

1 Lightly butter a shallow ovenproof dish or roasting pan. Lay the trout fillets in the dish, season lightly, and drizzle with 1 tablespoon of the oil. Bake in a preheated oven, 375°F, for 5 minutes.

2 Heat the remaining oil in a skillet and fry the pine nuts and onion for about 3 minutes until beginning to brown. Stir in the garlic and spinach, and mix together until the spinach has wilted.

3 Spoon the mixture over the trout and sprinkle with the cheese. Return to the oven for an additional 6–8 minutes until the fish is cooked through.

TIP

Trout is quick to cook and makes a lighter alternative to salmon in this quickly assembled supper dish. Buy ready-prepared trout fillets to save you the trouble of filleting and boning the whole fish.

Energy: 358 kcals/1490 kJ   **Protein:** 35 g
Carbohydrate: 3 g   **Fat:** 23 g   **Fiber:** 2 g
Calcium: 210 mg   **Iron:** 3 mg

Mediterranean lamb casserole

Serves 6 • Preparation: 20 minutes **• Cooking:** about 1½ hours

2 lb lean lamb, diced

2 lb tomatoes, skinned

1 medium eggplant

2 red onions

6 tablespoons olive oil

3 red bell peppers, seeded
and cut into chunks

2 zucchini, thickly sliced

4 garlic cloves, sliced

3 tablespoons sun-dried
tomato paste

6 rosemary sprigs

salt and pepper

1 Pat the lamb dry on paper towels and season lightly. Roughly chop the tomatoes. Cut the eggplant into small chunks. Cut the onions into thin wedges.

2 Heat 3 tablespoons of the oil in a large skillet or sauté pan and fry the meat in batches until deep golden. Remove from the pan and drain any excess fat. Add the onions to the pan and fry until golden, then remove from the pan and set aside.

3 Add the remaining oil to the pan with the eggplant, peppers, and zucchini, and fry for 5–10 minutes until lightly browned.

4 Return the meat and onions to the pan with the garlic, tomatoes, tomato paste, rosemary, and seasoning. Bring to a boil, reduce the heat, and cover with a lid. Cook gently, stirring occasionally, for about 1 hour until the lamb is tender and the vegetables are pulpy. Serve hot with rice, polenta, or new potatoes.

TIP

This dish freezes well. Pack into ovenproof or foil dishes and freeze for up to 3 months. Defrost overnight in the refrigerator.

Energy: 488 kcals/2036 kJ **Protein:** 38 g
Carbohydrate: 16 g **Fat:** 30 g **Fiber:** 5 g
Calcium: 52 mg **Iron:** 5 mg

Loin of pork with lentils

Serves 5–6 • **Preparation:** 15 minutes • **Cooking:** about 1½ hours

¾ cup Puy lentils

1¾ lb pork loin, skinned, boned, and rolled

2 tablespoons olive oil

2 large onions, sliced

3 garlic cloves, sliced

1 tablespoon finely chopped fresh rosemary

1¼ cups chicken or vegetable stock

8 oz baby carrots, scrubbed and left whole

salt and pepper

1 Put the lentils in a pan, cover with water, and bring to a boil. Boil rapidly for 10 minutes, then drain and set aside.

2 Sprinkle the pork with salt and pepper. Heat the oil in a large heavy skillet and brown the meat on all sides. Transfer to a casserole dish and add the lentils.

3 Add the onions to the pan and fry for 5 minutes. Add the garlic, rosemary, and stock, and bring to a boil. Pour over the meat and lentils and cover with a lid. Cook in a preheated oven, 350°F, for 1 hour.

4 Add the carrots and seasoning and return to the oven for an additional 20–30 minutes until the pork and lentils are tender. Drain the meat, transfer to a serving platter, and carve thin slices. Serve with the lentils and juices.

TIP

This flavorsome dish is good at any time of year: in winter served with heaps of roast potatoes and wintry vegetables, or in summer with buttery new potatoes.

   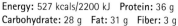

Energy: 527 kcals/2200 kJ   **Protein:** 36 g
Carbohydrate: 28 g   **Fat:** 31 g   **Fiber:** 3 g
Calcium: 80 mg   **Iron:** 5 mg

Spiced beef with spinach

Serves 4–5 • Preparation: 15 minutes • Cooking: 1½ hours

12 cardamom pods

2 teaspoons cumin seeds

2 teaspoons coriander seeds

1½ lb lean braising beef, diced

3 tablespoons vegetable oil

2 onions, chopped

½ teaspoon ground turmeric

½ inch piece fresh ginger root,
  peeled and finely chopped

1 mild red chili, seeded
  and sliced

4 garlic cloves, thinly sliced

2 teaspoons superfine sugar

13 oz can chopped tomatoes

¾ cup beef or chicken stock

6 cups baby spinach

salt and pepper

1 Crush the cardamom pods using a mortar and pestle to release the seeds. Discard the pods. Add the cumin and coriander and crush the seeds fairly finely.

2 Discard any excess fat from the beef and season lightly. Heat the oil in a large, heavy saucepan and fry the beef until it is browned. Add the onions, the crushed spices, and turmeric and fry for 5 minutes, stirring.

3 Add the ginger, chili, garlic, sugar, tomatoes, and stock, and bring to a boil. Reduce the heat, cover with a lid, and simmer very gently for about 1½ hours until the beef is tender.

4 Pack the spinach into the pan and cover with the lid. Cook for about 5 minutes until the spinach has wilted. Stir the spinach into the sauce, season to taste, and serve.

TIP

If you do not have a good selection of spices or simply want a short-cut version, use 2 teaspoons of medium curry paste instead of the separate spices.

Energy: 390 kcals/1640 kJ **Protein:** 43 g
Carbohydrate: 14 g **Fat:** 18 g **Fiber:** 5 g
Calcium: 193 mg **Iron:** 7 mg

Summer roast chicken

Serves 4 • Preparation: 15 minutes • Cooking: 1¼ hours

2¼ lb chicken

1 small stalk lemon grass

½ cup cream cheese

2 garlic cloves, crushed

2 tablespoons chopped chives

1 tablespoon chopped thyme

2 tablespoons chopped flat
  leaf parsley

1 small lemon, cut
  into wedges

1 lime, cut into wedges

salt and pepper

extra herbs, to garnish

VARIATION

Almost any herb can be used
in this recipe: try tarragon,
rosemary, fennel, or dill weed.

1 Wash the chicken and pat it dry with paper towels.
Using your fingers, loosen the skin away from the
breast meat and the tops of the thighs.

2 Trim and very finely chop the lemon grass. Beat the
cream cheese in a bowl with the lemon grass, garlic,
herbs, and a little seasoning. Using a teaspoon, pack
the stuffing under the chicken skin, pushing it as far
over the chicken thighs as you can reach without
tearing the skin. Push the skin back in place,
spreading the stuffing in an even layer.

3 Put the chicken in a roasting pan. Roast in a
preheated oven, 375°F, for 1¼ hours, adding the
lemon and lime wedges for the last 30 minutes of
the cooking time. To test that the chicken is cooked
through, pierce the thickest part of the thigh with a
skewer—the juices should run clear.

4 Carve the chicken and serve garnished with the
roasted lemon and lime and extra herbs.

TIP

If you want to make a light gravy, pour a little wine
or stock into the roasting pan and cook briefly over
a gentle heat until bubbling.

Energy: 473 kcals/1960 kJ Protein: 35 g
Carbohydrate: 0 g Fat: 37 g Fiber: 0 g
Calcium: 47 mg Iron: 1 mg

Thai coconut chicken

Serves 4 • **Preparation:** 20 minutes • **Cooking:** 45 minutes

1 green chili, seeded
and roughly chopped

1 small onion, roughly
chopped

3 garlic cloves, chopped

3 cups fresh cilantro

2 teaspoons Thai fish sauce

¼ teaspoon ground turmeric

1 stalk lemon grass,
roughly chopped

grated zest and juice of 1 lime

2 teaspoons superfine sugar

½ inch piece fresh ginger root,
roughly chopped

4 skinned, boneless
chicken breasts

1 tablespoon refined
peanut oil

2 cups chicken stock

1¾ cups coconut milk

salt and pepper

roughly chopped cilantro,
to garnish

1 To make the curry paste, put the chili, onion, garlic, cilantro, fish sauce, turmeric, lemon grass, lime zest and juice, sugar, and ginger in a food processor or blender and process until smooth, scraping the mixture down from the sides of the bowl when necessary.

2 Cut the chicken into small pieces and season lightly. Heat the oil in a large saucepan and gently fry the chicken for 5 minutes.

3 Put the stock and curry mixture in a separate pan and bring to a boil. Cook uncovered for 15–20 minutes until most of the liquid has evaporated.

4 Add the chicken and coconut milk and cook for about 20 minutes until the chicken is very tender. Garnish with cilantro and serve with fragrant rice or noodles.

Energy: 214 kcals/900 kJ   **Protein:** 29 g
Carbohydrate: 10 g   **Fat:** 7 g   **Fiber:** 0 g
Calcium: 60 mg   **Iron:** 1 mg

Mushroom risotto

Serves 4 • **Preparation:** 10 minutes • **Cooking:** about 30 minutes

¼ cup butter

1 tablespoon olive oil

2 medium onions, finely chopped

8 oz chestnut mushrooms, thinly sliced

1 celery stick, chopped

2 cups risotto rice

2 garlic cloves, crushed

⅔ cup white wine

4 cups chicken or vegetable stock

1 cup freshly grated Parmesan cheese

salt and pepper

VARIATION

If you prefer not to include the wine, simply substitute additional stock.

1 Melt half the butter with the oil in a large, heavy saucepan. Add the onions and fry gently for 2–3 minutes until softened. Add the chopped mushrooms and fry quickly for 2 minutes. Drain the mushrooms and set aside.

2 Add the celery, rice, and garlic, and cook, stirring, for 1 minute. Add the wine and continue to cook until it has evaporated.

3 Add 3 cups of the stock and cook uncovered, stirring frequently, for 20–25 minutes until the rice is tender and creamy, but still retains a little bite. Add more stock if necessary—the risotto should remain very juicy.

4 Stir in the mushrooms, half the cheese, the remaining butter, and seasoning to taste. Serve immediately with the remaining cheese sprinkled on top.

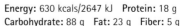

Energy: 630 kcals/2647 kJ   **Protein:** 18 g
Carbohydrate: 88 g   **Fat:** 23 g   **Fiber:** 5 g
Calcium: 335 mg   **Iron:** 2 mg

Roasted vegetable and red bean stew

Serves 5–6 • **Preparation:** 20 minutes, plus overnight soaking • **Cooking:** about 1¼ hours

1½ cups red kidney beans

2 lb butternut squash

3 large red onions, cut into thin wedges

3 zucchini, thickly sliced

1 medium eggplant, about 12 oz, cut into chunks

3 tablespoons olive oil

4 cups vegetable stock

3 garlic cloves, sliced

2 tablespoons chopped fresh oregano

3 bay leaves

2 tablespoons ground paprika

8 oz chestnut mushrooms, quartered

salt and pepper

sour cream, to serve (optional)

1 Soak the beans overnight in plenty of cold water. Drain, cover with fresh water, and bring to a boil. Boil rapidly for 10 minutes, then drain.

2 Meanwhile, halve the squash, discard the seeds, and cut away the skin. Cut the flesh into chunks and put in a large roasting pan with the onions, zucchini, and eggplant. Drizzle with the oil, add a little seasoning, and roast in a preheated oven, 425°F, for about 1 hour, turning the vegetables occasionally until deep golden.

3 Meanwhile, put the beans in a large saucepan. Add the stock, garlic, herbs, and paprika, and bring to a boil. Reduce the heat, cover, and simmer gently for 30–40 minutes until the beans are tender.

4 Tip the roasted vegetables into the pan with the mushrooms and cook for an additional 5 minutes until heated through. Serve in bowls, topped with spoonfuls of sour cream, if desired.

Energy: 350 kcals/1490 kJ   **Protein:** 18 g
Carbohydrate: 55 g   **Fat:** 9 g   **Fiber:** 17 g
Calcium: 215 mg   **Iron:** 7 mg

Strawberry meringue roulade

Serves 6-8 • **Preparation:** 20 minutes, plus cooling • **Cooking:** 30 minutes

4 medium egg whites

½ cup superfine sugar

1 teaspoon white wine vinegar

1 teaspoon vanilla extract

¼ cup slivered almonds

2¼ cups ripe strawberries

⅔ cup heavy cream

4 tablespoons orange-flavored liqueur

confectioners' sugar for dusting

VARIATION

This luxurious dessert can be adapted for any fruit, depending on what is in season—plump summer berries, juicy soft peaches and plums, or a range of tropical fruits all make a delicious filling.

1 Line a 13 x 9 inch jelly roll pan with parchment paper. Beat the egg whites in a thoroughly clean bowl until stiff. Gradually beat in the sugar, a tablespoonful at a time, beating well after each addition until the mixture is stiff and glossy. Beat in the vinegar and vanilla extract.

2 Turn the mixture into the prepared pan and spread to an even layer. Sprinkle with the slivered almonds. Bake in a preheated oven at 325°F, for about 30 minutes until the surface is turning pale golden. Allow to cool in the pan.

3 Sprinkle a sheet of parchment paper with a little extra sugar and invert the meringue onto the paper. Peel away the lining paper from the meringue.

4 Thinly slice the strawberries. Whip the cream with the liqueur until it just holds its shape. Spread to within ½ inch of the edges of the meringue. Sprinkle with the strawberries and roll up, starting from a short edge.

5 Slide onto a serving plate and chill until ready to serve, lightly dusted with confectioners' sugar.

Energy: 277 kcals/1156 kJ   Protein: 4 g
Carbohydrate: 30 g   Fat: 14 g   Fiber: 2 g
Calcium: 35 mg   Iron: <1 mg

Apricot and marzipan tart

Serves 6–8 • Preparation: 30 minutes • **Cooking:** 40 minutes

2 cups white rice flour

2 teaspoons ground cinnamon

½ cup firm unsalted butter

1 egg yolk

½ cup grated cooking apple (about 1 medium apple)

¼ cup plus 2 tablespoons superfine sugar

½ cup confectioners' sugar

1¼ cups ground almonds

finely grated zest of 1 orange

1 egg, beaten

1¼ lb ripe apricots

¼ cup slivered almonds

4 tablespoons apricot jelly

1 Put the flour and cinnamon in a bowl with the butter, cut into small pieces, and blend with the fingertips. Stir in the egg yolk, grated apple, and 2 tablespoons of superfine sugar, and mix to a dough.

2 Break off pieces of dough, flatten them between your hands and press into a 9 inch round removable-bottomed pan so that the pan is lined in sections. Trim off any excess around the top.

3 Mix together the remaining superfine sugar, confectioners' sugar, ground almonds, and orange zest. Add the egg and mix to a paste. Pack the paste into the tart shell. Halve and pit the apricots and sprinkle over the filling. Sprinkle with the slivered almonds.

4 Bake in a preheated oven at 200°F, for about 40 minutes until the pastry is golden and the apricots are tender.

5 While the tart is cooking, melt the jelly in a small pan with 1 tablespoon of water and use to glaze the apricots. Serve warm or cold with pouring cream.

Energy: 610 kcals/2547 kJ   Protein: 11 g
Carbohydrate: 70 g   Fat: 32 g   Fiber: 6 g
Calcium: 122 mg   Iron: 3 mg

Caramel fruit pudding

Serves 6 • Preparation: 20 minutes • Cooking: 1½ hours

¼ cup unsalted butter

¼ cup light brown sugar

2 bananas, sliced

2 pears, cored and
  chopped

1 cup no-soak dried
  apricots, chopped

finely grated zest and
  juice of 1 lemon

PUDDING MIX

½ cup light brown sugar

½ cup unsalted butter,
  softened

2 eggs

½ cup gluten-free flour

1 teaspoon Gluten-free baking
  powder (see page 42)

1 teaspoon ground mixed
  spice

3 cups gluten-free bread
  crumbs

1 Grease and base line a 6 cup pudding basin. Dice the
  butter and mix with the sugar, half the prepared fruit,
  and the lemon zest and juice. Tip into the basin.

2 For the pudding mix, put the sugar, butter, eggs,
  flour, baking powder, and spice in a bowl and beat
  until smooth (don't worry if the mixture curdles at
  this stage). Stir in the bread crumbs and the
  remaining fruit.

3 Spoon the mixture over the fruit in the basin and level
  the surface. Cover with a double thickness of waxed
  paper, pleated in the center to allow for expansion,
  and tie under the rim with string. Trim off the excess
  paper, then cover with foil, scrunching the edges
  under the rim to seal the pudding.

4 Place in a roasting pan and half-fill with boiling water.
  Overwrap with a large sheet of foil and transfer to a
  preheated oven, 325°F. Bake for 1½ hours.

5 Carefully take the basin from the pan and remove
  the waxed paper. Tip the pudding onto a serving
  plate and cut in wedges. Serve with cream, ice
  cream, or yogurt.

Energy: 514 kcals/2155 kJ   **Protein:** 5 g
Carbohydrate: 67 g   **Fat:** 27 g   **Fiber:** 7 g
Calcium: 76 mg   **Iron:** 2 mg

Sweet pancakes with citrus sauce

Serves 4–6 • Preparation: 25 minutes • Cooking: about 20 minutes

2 oranges

3 tablespoons butter

½ cup rice flour

3 tablespoons superfine sugar

6 tablespoons milk

2 eggs, separated

oil for frying

2 tablespoons lemon juice

2 tablespoons orange liqueur (optional)

6 scoops vanilla ice cream

1 Finely grate the zest from 1 orange. Melt 1 tablespoon of the butter. Put the flour, orange zest, melted butter, 1 tablespoon of sugar, the milk, and egg yolks in a bowl and beat until smooth.

2 In a separate bowl, beat the egg whites until frothy and just beginning to hold their shape. Add to the bowl and stir in until combined.

3 Heat a little oil in a medium crêpe pan, drain off the excess and pour a little of the batter into the pan so that it spreads to about 6 inches in diameter. (If the batter is too thick spread it with the back of a spoon.) Once golden on the underside, turn the pancake and cook until set enough to slide out of the pan. Keep warm. Make the remainder, brushing the pan with a little more oil each time.

4 Squeeze the juice from the 2 oranges. Melt the remaining butter and sugar in a skillet until the sugar has dissolved. Add the orange and lemon juice and let the mixture bubble for about 2 minutes until syrupy. Stir in the liqueur if using.

5 Fold the pancakes into quarters and place on serving plates. Pour the sauce over and serve immediately with ice cream.

Energy: 460 kcals/1933 kJ   Protein: 9 g
Carbohydrate: 50 g   Fat: 26 g   Fiber: 1 g
Calcium: 204 mg   Iron: 1 mg

Cherry and almond clafoutis

Serves 4 • Preparation: 10 minutes **• Cooking:** 25 minutes

14 oz can pitted black cherries

2 eggs

1 egg yolk

¼ cup superfine sugar

2 tablespoons butter, melted

¼ cup ground almonds

1 teaspoon vanilla extract

¾ cup milk

6 tablespoons heavy cream

confectioners' sugar for
dusting

1 Lightly butter a 4 cup shallow ovenproof dish. Drain the cherries thoroughly and scatter in the dish.

2 Beat the eggs with the yolk and sugar until slightly thickened and frothy. Stir in the butter, ground almonds, vanilla, milk, and cream to make a smooth batter.

3 Pour the mixture over the cherries, then bake in a preheated oven, 375°F, for 25–30 minutes until golden and only just setting in the middle. Dust with confectioners' sugar and serve warm.

VARIATION

During their short season, fresh cherries can be used instead of tinned or jarred. Allow about 1¼ cups and remember to remove the pits first.

Energy: 398 kcals/1697 kJ **Protein:** 8 g
Carbohydrate: 34 g **Fat:** 27 g **Fiber:** 2 g
Calcium: 115 mg **Iron:** 4 mg

Christmas pudding

Serves 12 • **Preparation:** 20 minutes • **Cooking:** 4 hours, plus 2 hours reheating

1½ cups dried figs or dates, chopped

1½ cups no-soak prunes, chopped

6 cups mixed dried fruit

3 pieces stem ginger, finely chopped

½ cup dark brown sugar

finely grated zest and juice of 1 orange

3 cups gluten-free bread crumbs

¾ stick unsalted butter, chilled

3 eggs

6 tablespoons medium sherry

superfine sugar for sprinkling

1 Mix together the fruits, ginger, sugar, orange zest and juice, and bread crumbs in a large bowl.

2 Grate the butter directly over the bowl, stirring in frequently as you work so that it does not cake together. Add the eggs and sherry, mixing until evenly combined.

3 Lightly grease and line the base of an 8 cup pudding basin, then pack the mixture in, leveling the surface with the back of a spoon.

4 Cover with a double thickness of waxed paper, pleated in the center to allow for expansion, and tie under the rim with string. Trim off the excess paper, then cover with foil, scrunching the edges under the rim to seal.

5 Put the pudding in a large, heavy saucepan and add boiling water to halfway up the sides of the basin. Cover with a lid and steam gently for 4 hours, topping up with more boiling water if necessary. Allow to cool.

6 To reheat, steam as above for 2 hours. Loosen the edges of the pudding with a knife, then turn on to a serving plate. Serve sprinkled with superfine sugar.

Energy: 468 kcals/1980 kJ   **Protein:** 5 g
Carbohydrate: 96 g   **Fat:** 9 g   **Fiber:** 11 g
Calcium: 137 mg   **Iron:** 4 mg

Coffee and almond trifle

Serves 6 • Preparation: 15 minutes

6 tablespoons strong black coffee, cooled

6 tablespoons Kahlua or other coffee-flavored liqueur

¾ cup full-fat cream cheese

2 cups good-quality, creamy custard

7 oz homemade (see page 118) or ready-made almond macaroons

¼ cup coarsely grated semisweet or milk chocolate

¼ cup slivered almonds, lightly toasted

1 Mix the coffee with the liqueur in a jug.

2 Beat the cream cheese in a bowl to soften, then gradually beat in the custard until the mixture is completely smooth.

3 Arrange half the macaroons in the base of a 6 cup glass serving dish and drizzle with half the coffee mixture. Put the remaining macaroons in a single layer on a plate and drizzle the remaining syrup over them.

4 Sprinkle half the chocolate and half the almonds over the macaroons in the bowl. Spoon over half the cheese mixture.

5 Reserve a tablespoonful each of the chocolate and almonds for decoration. Layer the syrup steeped macaroons, chocolate, and almonds in the dish. Pile the remaining cheese mixture on top and sprinkle with the reserved chocolate and almonds. Chill until ready to serve.

Energy: 500 kcals/2093 kJ   **Protein:** 8 g
Carbohydrate: 45 g   **Fat:** 31 g   **Fiber:** 2 g
Calcium: 186 mg   **Iron:** 1 mg

Summer pudding

Serves 6–8 • Preparation: 20 minutes, plus chilling • **Cooking:** 5 minutes

10 slices white gluten-free bread

6 cups mixed summer fruits, such as red currants, black currants, blackberries, strawberries, or raspberries

½ cup superfine sugar

pouring cream or thick yogurt, to serve

1 Put three bread slices to one side. Use the rest to line the base and sides of a 5 cup pudding basin, overlapping them to make a sealed outer layer.

2 Remove the stalks from the red currants and black currants, if using, and hull the strawberries, halving any large ones. Tip into a large heavy saucepan and add the sugar. Heat gently for about 5 minutes, stirring frequently until the juices flow and the sugar has dissolved.

3 Using a large spoon, fill the bread-lined basin with the fruit, reserving any juice left in the pan. Place the remaining bread over the surface, trimming to fit. The bread should be soaked in juices, so pour over a little more juice if the bread seems dry. Cover and chill for at least 8 hours or overnight. Pour any remaining juice into a small pitcher.

4 To serve, loosen around the edges with a knife and invert onto a flat plate. Serve in wedges with cream or yogurt and extra juice if desired.

Energy: 295 kcals/1240 kJ   Protein: 3 g
Carbohydrate: 51 g   Fat: 10 g   Fiber: 8 g
Calcium: 76 mg   Iron: 1 mg

Pannacotta with blueberry sauce

Serves 6 • Preparation: 25 minutes

1½ teaspoons powdered
  gelatin or vegetarian
  gelling agent

1¼ cups mascarpone
  cheese

1¼ cups heavy cream

finely grated zest of 1 orange
  plus 2 teaspoons juice

½ cup superfine sugar

2 teaspoons vanilla extract

SAUCE

2 cups blueberries

1 tablespoon confectioners'
  sugar

1 Sprinkle the powdered gelatin over 3 tablespoons of water in a small bowl and set aside. Lightly oil six small dariole or individual metal pudding molds.

2 Put the mascarpone in a saucepan with the cream, orange zest, sugar, and vanilla, and bring just to a boil. Remove from the heat and add the gelatin. Stir thoroughly until the gelatin has completely dissolved.

3 Pour the cream mixture into the molds and chill for several hours, or overnight until set.

4 Put the blueberries in a bowl and pierce all over with a fork to let the juices run a little. Add the confectioners' sugar and orange juice, and mix together. Chill until ready to serve.

5 To serve, loosen the edges of the molds with a knife and then shake them out onto individual plates. Spoon the blueberry sauce all around.

Energy: 530 kcals/2208 kJ   Protein: 5 g
Carbohydrate: 30 g   Fat: 44 g   Fiber: 3 g
Calcium: 53 mg   Iron: 1 mg

Lemony cornmeal cake

Serves 6 • **Preparation:** 10 minutes • **Cooking:** 30 minutes

¾ cup unsalted butter, softened

1 cup superfine sugar

1 cup ground almonds

2 eggs, beaten

finely grated zest and juice of 3 lemons

¾ cup corn flour

½ cup gluten-free all-purpose flour

½ teaspoon Gluten-free baking powder (see page 42)

2 tablespoons slivered almonds

1 Grease and line a 6 inch spring-form pan with waxed paper. Beat together the butter and ¾ cup of the sugar until pale and creamy. Stir in the almonds, eggs, and zest and juice of 1 lemon.

2 Add the flours and baking powder, and stir in gently until combined. Turn into the pan, level the surface, and sprinkle with the slivered almonds. Bake in a preheated oven, 350°F, for about 30 minutes until risen and just firm.

3 Meanwhile, put the remaining lemon zest and juice in a small pan with the remaining sugar and heat gently until the sugar dissolves. Spoon over the cake and serve warm.

TIP
This crumbly almond spongecake, dripping with a tangy, lemon syrup, is great with a cup of coffee. Alternatively, top with cream or yogurt for a tempting dessert.

116 Cakes and bakes

Energy: 598 kcals/2490 kJ   **Protein:** 9 g
Carbohydrate: 55 g   **Fat:** 39 g   **Fiber:** 3 g
Calcium: 104 mg   **Iron:** 2 mg

Almond macaroons

Makes about 20 • **Preparation:** 10 minutes • **Cooking:** 15–20 minutes

2 egg whites

½ cup superfine sugar

1 cup ground almonds

blanched almonds, to decorate

1 Line a large baking sheet with parchment paper. Beat the egg whites until stiff. Gradually beat in the sugar, a spoonful at a time, until the mixture is thick and glossy. Stir in the ground almonds.

2 Spoon the mixture into a large plastic bag, squeezing it gently into a corner. Snip off the corner of the bag so the mixture can be piped onto the baking sheet.

3 Pipe small rounds about 1½ inches in diameter, spacing them slightly apart. Press a blanched almond into the top of each one.

4 Bake in a preheated oven, 350°F, for 15–20 minutes until only just firm. Leave on the paper to cool.

TIP

If you would prefer not to pipe the mixture, simply drop spoonfuls onto the baking sheet. These classic, chewy teatime favorites can be served as they are or scribbled with melted dark chocolate.

Energy: 62 kcals/260 kJ Protein: 2 g
Carbohydrate: 6 g Fat: 4 g Fiber: 1 g
Calcium: 16 mg Iron: 0 mg

Lemon-glazed shortbread

Serves 10–12 • **Preparation:** 10 minutes • **Cooking:** 35 minutes

1 cup ground rice

1 cup gluten-free flour

finely grated zest of 1 lemon plus 2½ teaspoons juice

½ cup lightly salted butter

¼ cup superfine sugar

¾ cup confectioners' sugar

VARIATION

You can use orange instead of the lemon, or leave out the fruit and simply dust generously with confectioners' sugar instead.

1 Grease an 8 inch round, removable-bottomed layer pan. Put the ground rice, flour, and lemon zest in a food processor. Add the butter, cut into small pieces, and process until the mixture resembles bread crumbs.

2 Add the superfine sugar and blend again until the mixture starts to bind together. (Alternatively, put the rice, flour, and lemon zest in a bowl, add the butter, and blend with fingertips before adding the sugar.) Turn into the pan and press down with the fingertips until the surface is level.

3 Bake in a preheated oven, 325°F, for about 35 minutes until pale golden. Leave in the pan for 5 minutes, then lift the base out of the pan and slide the shortbread onto a wire rack. Mark into small wedges.

4 Beat together the lemon juice and confectioners' sugar to make a thin icing with the consistency of pouring cream. Drizzle over the shortbread and allow to set. Store in an airtight container for up to 4 days.

Energy: 200 kcals/855 kJ **Protein:** 1 g
Carbohydrate: 32 g **Fat:** 8 g **Fiber:** 0 g
Calcium: 5 mg **Iron:** 0 mg

Chunky rich fruit cake

Serves 24 • Preparation: 20 minutes **• Cooking:** about 1¼ hours

1¼ cups apple juice

4 teaspoons active dry yeast

1 cooking apple, cored and roughly chopped

1 cup gluten-free flour

2 cups rice flour

2 teaspoons Gluten-free baking powder (see page 42)

1 tablespoon ground mixed spice

2 tablespoons butter, melted

1 medium carrot, finely grated

1¾ cups luxury mixed dried fruit

⅔ cup no-soak prunes, chopped

⅔ cup no-soak dried apricots, chopped

1 cup blanched almonds, roughly chopped

1 Grease and line an 8 inch round or 7 inch square cake pan. Gently warm the apple juice in a small pan until tepid. Remove from the heat and sprinkle with the yeast. Leave for 5 minutes until the mixture is frothy. Transfer to a food processor or blender, add the apple, and process until the apple is almost smooth.

2 Put the flours, baking powder, and spice into a mixing bowl. Add the butter, carrot, and yeast mixture, and stir until combined.

3 Add all the dried fruit and the almonds, and stir well. Turn into the prepared pan and bake in a preheated oven, 325°F, for about 1¼ hours or until the surface is firm to the touch and a skewer inserted into the center comes out clean. Allow to cool in the tin.

4 Wrap tightly in foil and store in a cool place until needed.

TIP

For a special occasion, you can add alcohol to the recipe. After baking, pierce the surface of the cake with a skewer and drizzle with 4–5 tablespoons of brandy, rum, or orange liqueur. Wrap and store.

Energy: 153 kcals/640 kJ Protein: 3 g
Carbohydrate: 27 g Fat: 4 g Fiber: 3 g
Calcium: 40 mg Iron: 1 mg

Very chocolately brownies

Makes 18 • **Preparation:** 10 minutes • **Cooking:** 30 minutes

7 oz milk chocolate

7 oz semisweet chocolate

1 cup unsalted butter

3 eggs

¾ cup light brown sugar

¾ cup gluten-free flour

2 teaspoons Gluten-free baking powder (see page 42)

1 cup walnut pieces

VARIATION

Chop the walnuts finely if you prefer, or substitute almonds or macadamia nuts for a milder flavor.

1 Grease and line an 11 x 8 inch shallow baking pan with parchment paper. Chop the milk chocolate into small chunks. Melt the semisweet chocolate with the butter in a small bowl set over hot water.

2 Beat together the eggs and sugar until turning foamy. Stir in the melted chocolate mixture.

3 Sift the flour and baking powder into the bowl. Add the chopped chocolate and walnut pieces and fold the ingredients together gently. Pour the mixture into the baking pan.

4 Bake in a preheated oven at 375°F, for 30 minutes until a sugary crust has formed on the surface but the mixture gives slightly underneath (it will firm up slightly as it cools, so avoid the temptation to cook for longer). Allow to cool in the pan.

5 Cut into squares and store in an airtight container in a cool place for up to 6 days.

Energy: 343 kcals/1428 kJ **Protein:** 5 g
Carbohydrate: 28 g **Fat:** 24 g **Fiber:** 1 g
Calcium: 56 mg **Iron:** 1 mg

Fruited teacake

Makes 8 slices • **Preparation:** 5 minutes • **Cooking:** 40 minutes

1¾ cups mixed dried fruit

⅓ cup dark brown sugar

finely grated zest of
1 orange

⅔ cup orange juice

1 cup gluten-free flour

½ teaspoon Gluten-free baking
powder (see page 42)

1 egg, lightly beaten

1 Grease a 1 lb loaf pan. Put the dried fruit, sugar, orange zest and juice in a small, heavy saucepan. Bring to a boil and let the mixture bubble for about 5 minutes until the liquid is thickened and syrupy. Tip into a mixing bowl and leave for 10 minutes.

2 Add the flour, baking powder, and egg, and stir until combined. Turn into the pan and bake in a preheated oven, 350°F, for about 40 minutes until slightly risen and firm to the touch. Transfer to a wire rack to cool.

VARIATION

For flavor variations, try lemon or grapefruit instead of the orange and add a little spice such as ground cinnamon, cloves, or ginger.

Energy: 200 kcals/853 kJ **Protein:** 3 g
Carbohydrate: 48 g **Fat:** 1 g **Fiber:** 3 g
Calcium: 42 mg **Iron:** 1 mg

Rich chocolate and hazelnut gateau

Serves 10–12 • **Preparation:** 20 minutes, plus cooling • **Cooking:** 30 minutes

7 oz semisweet chocolate

5 tablespoons milk

¾ cup very soft unsalted butter

¾ cup superfine sugar

1½ cups ground hazelnuts

½ cup gluten-free flour

5 eggs, separated

FROSTING

3½ oz semisweet chocolate

1 tablespoon butter

¼ cup blanched hazelnuts, toasted and roughly chopped

1 Grease and line a 9 inch round cake pan. Melt the chocolate with the milk, stirring occasionally until smooth.

2 Transfer to a mixing bowl and add the butter, sugar, ground nuts, flour, and egg yolks. Stir until well combined.

3 In a separate bowl, beat the egg whites until peaking. Using a large metal spoon, transfer a quarter of the whites to the chocolate mixture and fold in. Fold in the remainder.

4 Turn into the prepared pan and level the surface. Bake in a preheated oven, 350°F, for 30 minutes or until the surface feels just firm to the touch. Allow to cool in the pan before turning out.

5 To decorate the cake, melt together the chocolate and butter and spread over the top. Sprinkle the chopped hazelnuts around the top edges of the cake. Allow to set.

Energy: 560 kcals/2330 kJ   **Protein:** 8 g
Carbohydrate: 44 g   **Fat:** 40 g   **Fiber:** 2 g
Calcium: 67 mg   **Iron:** 2 mg

Index

Acknowledgments

Photographic Acknowledgments in Source Order

Special photography ©Octopus Publishing Group
Limited/Craig Robertson.

Other photography:
Corbis UK Limited/David Raymer 37.
Getty Images/Grant V. Faint 7; /Gerd George 28; /Bay Hippisley 4;
/Howard Kingsnorth 20; /Tony Latham 11 top right; /Frederic Tousche 6.
Octopus Publishing Group Limited/Stephen Conroy 17 detail 11;
/David Jordan 16 detail 5, 23, 27, 29, 35; /Graham Kirk 17 detail 14;
/William Lingwood 10; /Neil Mersh 30; /Sean Myers 17 detail 9; /Peter
Pugh-Cook 12, 17 detail 13, 22, 24, 25; /William Reavell 5 top left, 5
bottom right, 5 bottom left, 5 bottom center, 8 bottom, 16 detail 1, 16
detail 2, 16 detail 3, 16 detail 4, 16 detail 6, 17 detail 8, 17 detail 10, 17
detail 12, 18 bottom left, 20 bottom left, 21 top left, 21 bottom left, 26;
/Gareth Sambidge 32; /Simon Smith 15 detail 7, 21 center; /Mark
Winwood 31.
Science Photo Library/Sheila Terry 19 top.

Executive Editor Nicola Hill
Editor Kate Tuckett
Executive Art Editor Joanna MacGregor
Designer Darren Southern
Production Controller Nosheen Shan
Special Photography Craig Robertson
Home Economist Sarah O'Brien
Picture Researcher Christine Junemann